The Clintons'
anti-working-class
record

ALSO BY JACK BARNES

BOOKS & PAMPHLETS
Are They Rich Because They're Smart? Class, Privilege, and
   Learning Under Capitalism (2016)
Malcolm X, Black Liberation, and the Road
   to Workers Power (2009)
Cuba and the Coming American Revolution (2007)
The Changing Face of US Politics (2002)
Their Trotsky and Ours (2002)
The Working Class and the Transformation of Learning (2000)
Capitalism's World Disorder (1999)
Malcolm X Talks to Young People (1965)

FROM THE PAGES OF 'NEW INTERNATIONAL'
Capitalism's Long Hot Winter Has Begun (2005)
Our Politics Start with the World (2005)
US Imperialism Has Lost the Cold War (1998)
The Opening Guns of World War III (1991)
Politics of Economics: Che Guevara and
   Marxist Continuity (1991)
The Fight for a Workers and Farmers Government
   in the US (1985)

COLLECTIONS AND INTRODUCTIONS
Teamster Rebellion/Dobbs (2004)
The History of American Trotskyism/Cannon (2002)
The Eastern Airlines Strike/E. Mailhot (1991)
FBI on Trial (1988)

The Clintons' anti-working-class record

WHY WASHINGTON FEARS WORKING PEOPLE

JACK BARNES

PATHFINDER

NEW YORK LONDON MONTREAL SYDNEY

EDITED BY: Steve Clark

ISBN 978-1-60488-098-4
Library of Congress Control Number 2017933700
Manufactured in the United States of America

First edition, 2016
Second edition, 2017

COVER DESIGN: Eva Braiman

COVER PHOTOS: Left: President William Clinton signs law fulfilling brutal pledge to "end welfare as we know it," August 22, 1996, on White House lawn. Also in photo are former recipients of Aid to Families with Dependent Children (AFDC): Penelope Howard (right); Janet Errel (at rear); and Lillie Harden (left), who introduced Clinton at ceremony.

In 2002, after suffering a stroke, Harden was denied Medicaid, which she'd gotten while receiving AFDC payments, and couldn't afford a $450 per month prescription. Asked by a journalist in 2005 about Clinton's pledge to exchange "welfare for work," Harden said that for her it "didn't pay off in the end." Harden died in 2014 at age 59. (J. Scott Applewhite/AP)

Right: President Barack Obama and Hillary Clinton with other top administration and Pentagon officials in White House war room during May 1, 2011, assault in which US Special Forces murdered Osama bin Laden. They are watching a video feed from a drone above the home in which bin Laden and his family were living in Abbottabad, Pakistan. (White House Press Office)

CARTOON ON PAGE 17: Reprinted with permission of *Grant's Interest Rate Observer*, copyright 2016.

PATHFINDER
www.pathfinderpress.com
E-mail: pathfinder@pathfinderpress.com

To

TOM FISKE
(1943–2015)

and

FRANK FORRESTAL
(1954–2015)

◈

Lifetime leaders
of the communist movement

For whom class and politics
were a unity

CONTENTS

Boxes, photos, and illustrations (next page)

Boxes, photos, and illustrations

ABOUT THE AUTHOR

 **JACK BARNES** is National Secretary of the Socialist Workers Party. He has been a member of the party's National Committee since 1963 and a national officer since 1969. He is a contributing editor of *New International* magazine.

Barnes joined the Young Socialist Alliance in December 1960, a few months after a trip to Cuba in July and August of that year. Following his return, he helped organize at Carleton College in Minnesota one of the largest and most active campus chapters of the Fair Play for Cuba Committee. In May 1961 he joined the Socialist Workers Party.

While organizer of the SWP in Chicago and YSA Midwest organizer, Barnes was a central leader of the successful four-year campaign to defend three YSA members in Bloomington, Indiana, indicted in May 1963 for "assembling" to advocate the overthrow of the State of Indiana by force and violence.

In 1965 he was elected YSA national chairman and became director of the SWP's and YSA's work to advance the growing movement against the Vietnam War. In January of that year he met twice with Malcolm X for an interview that was published in the *Young Socialist* magazine.

Since the mid-1970s Barnes has led the work of the Socialist Workers Party, and collaborated with others around the world, to build proletarian parties the large majority of whose members and leaders are industrial workers and trade unionists actively engaged in communist propaganda activity and political work in the working class. This course to forge parties advancing a revolutionary course toward workers power and the struggle for socialism worldwide is recorded in articles and collections of Barnes's speeches and writings, some of which are listed at the front of the book.

Introduction

"DEPLORABLES." "IRREDEEMABLE." Those were Hillary Clinton's contemptuous words for millions of working people in the United States living and trying to work amid capitalism's grinding decline.

This book is about those millions and others like us the world over. It is about why we are at the center of politics today, and will become more so in the months and years after the new US administration is sworn in on January 20, 2017.

Clinton's deeply held attitudes, blurted out in a rare unscripted moment to wealthy supporters during a Manhattan fund-raising event, revealed what millions of working people already know all too well. Workers and our families have lived for more than two decades with the consequences of the Clintons' occupancy of the White House, from 1993 to 2001, when they made the brutal drive to end "welfare as we know it" their hallmark. And when they pushed through legislation such as the grotesquely named "Anti-Terrorism and Effective Death Penalty Act," which has had a devastating impact on working-class families, especially those who are African American.

The Clintons' Anti-Working-Class Record: Why Washing-

ton Fears Working People by Jack Barnes, the National Secretary of the Socialist Workers Party, brings together in one place these and other chapters of the last twenty-five years of the profit-driven course of the Clintons and their fellow political servants of the US capitalist rulers.

Barnes describes the human toll on working people in the United States, including the gutting of the meager "social safety net" won in hard-fought battles by the US working class over decades. He explains what growing numbers of workers already sense is happening to us, no matter how vehemently the wealthy and powerful deny it. We are living through a slow-burning economic contraction and financial crisis—a global capitalist crisis not one of us has seen before.

And it's working people the world over who are carrying the burdens of that deepening social calamity.

As Clinton's words reveal, for the first time in decades, the US rulers and their government have begun *to fear* the working class. Not because there are yet massive workers struggles like those that forged the industrial unions in the 1930s, or the proletarian-based battles for Black rights in the 1950s and 1960s that defeated Jim Crow segregation and terror. There is as yet no broad working-class politicalization in the United States.

They fear us because they recognize that more and more working people are beginning to see that the bosses and their political parties have no "solutions" that don't further load the costs—monetary and human—of the crisis of *their* system on *us*. Since the 2008–09 financial crash and economic contraction, more and more workers and farmers are already engaged in a wide-ranging and angry discussion of this capitalist reality. Although no one can foresee the timing, the financial capitalists and well-paid professionals who serve them sense that mounting struggle—*class struggle*—lies ahead.

Neither Washington nor Wall Street has any course that can contain the explosive international ramifications of capitalism's banking and financial contradictions. Nor do any of their capitalist allies and competitors, from London to Berlin to Tokyo.

Not a single one of them is pursuing policies that can reverse the slump of capitalist production, trade, and hiring that is ravaging the lives and livelihoods of workers, working farmers, and our families. None can turn around today's shrinking of the active working class, the increasing age at which young people start independent productive lives, and the slowdown in the formation of families able to keep a roof overhead and food on the table.

Why? *Because there are no such policies.* What's happening in today's world is not the result of policy "failures" by the White House, Congress, Federal Reserve, or the more and more wretchedly politicized and self-important Supreme Court. It is the result of the workings of capitalism itself. And that's where we must aim our fire, not at scapegoats singled out by reactionary demagogues to divert our energies.

Pressing interest rates near zero (or below). Buying up huge quantities of government securities (and, down the road, corporate stocks and bonds). New "regulations" aimed at curbing banks and industries. A big increase in government deficit spending. Even giant outlays for war, such as the $5 trillion already poured into US military operations in Iraq, Afghanistan, and elsewhere just since 2001. Such policies may be able to *postpone* or temporarily *buffer* the effects of the next breakdown, but they cannot and will not *prevent* it. Let alone "kick-start" economic growth and employment.

Capitalism long ago became a global system. The US ruling families and their rivals in Europe and the Pacific engage in ceaseless efforts to maximize their own profits the world over. Growing carnage and the dispossession of millions of human beings is the result. From Afghanistan through Iraq, Syria, and Yemen; from Somalia and Sudan, across large swathes of Africa and beyond. The earth has become a sea of refugees, whose numbers and deprivations have not been seen since the end of World War II.

It's a world in which imperialist superexploitation breeds and perpetuates not only illiteracy and crushing levels of infant and maternal mortality but also terrifying epidemics of preventable disease. The Ebola crisis in West Africa in 2014, cholera in Haiti in 2010 and again in 2015 and 2016, the Zika virus across Latin America and the Caribbean, including the debt-enslaved US colony of Puerto Rico—these are but the most recent. Imperialism leaves hundreds of millions without potable water, sanitation, electricity, and food, from Guatemala to Bangladesh, from Nigeria to the Philippines.

Amid this growing domestic and international nightmare, politicians of both major capitalist parties, as well as the big-business media, work overtime to spread the smear campaign that working people in the United States in massive numbers are "racist, sexist, homophobic, xenophobic, Islamophobic, you name it," as Hillary Clinton put it during that September 2016 fund-raising speech. They are not only "deplorable," she said. Most importantly,

"They are irredeemable."

But what has been registered by the 2016 election campaign—in partial and distorted ways, as with all bourgeois electoral phenomena—has little to do with Donald Trump's crude demeaning of women, immigrants, Muslims, and others. That's not why millions of those Hillary Clinton considers "irredeemable" have voted for him. The truth is that even more have refused to vote either for her or for him.

What has been registered is something different: the bourgeois two-party system has, for so long, delivered nothing but crushed expectations. In 2016 millions are casting votes for what they hope may be a change. Many others have already decided in disgust to simply sit this one out, at least the top of the ballot.

Whether it's Trump's billions, or the hundreds of millions accumulated by the Clintons themselves and by their foundation in the fifteen years since they occupied the White House, the wealth of both bourgeois party candidates depends on the capitalist social relations they proudly promote. And the profits they take depend on *competition* and *division* among workers. Layoffs and unemployment. Multi-tier contracts and job combinations. Racist discrimination. Women's second-class status. The ever-present fear of cop brutality. Pariah conditions of immigrant labor and refugees. Bloody wars and military operations to protect US imperialist interests overseas. Without the cutthroat class relations inherent in capitalism, *billions of dollars* in super-profits pocketed by the employing class, year in and year out, would evaporate.

They grow wealthy by exploiting our labor and keeping us divided. It's the lawful workings of capitalist production and distribution—and the state power that defends exploitation and oppression—that corrode working-class solidarity.

That's what's deplorable.

◈

Whatever the outcome of the 2016 presidential and congressional elections, an unprecedented blow has been dealt to the stability of the capitalist party system in the United States. Since the consolidation more than a century ago of the Democratic and Republican parties' domination of bourgeois politics in the new rising imperialist power, there has been nothing comparable.

In order for the two-party system to function effectively for the rulers, there needs to be a "lesser evil." And the lesser evils need to alternate—a Democrat for a few terms, then a Republican, to and fro. That's how it has worked for decades as an effective pressure valve to let off anger among "the electorate."

But that's not what happened in 2016.

Never before have the presidential candidates of *both* major capitalist parties evoked such political distrust, disgust, and aversion among working people, youth, and broad layers of the lower middle class. The cartoon says it all. *Both signs are dead right!* There is no lesser evil.

And the crisis conditions that have produced this shakeup in the bourgeois two-party setup aren't going away. They are worsening.

What has been unprecedented in 2016 is the exposure of something the US ruling class has largely succeeded in obscuring for decades. It has shown in life that the bour-

GRANT'S INTEREST RATE OBSERVER/HERB BLAUSTEIN

geois electoral system in the United States is rigged—yes, rigged on behalf of the propertied owners and their large rent-collecting meritocracy. The big majority of the ruling families—often mistakenly labeled the "establishment," or "political elite," by those hoping to obscure their class character—made clear a few months before the November elections that they intended to use television, newspapers, and any stick they could get their hands on to ensure Trump's defeat.

The squashing of Bernie Sanders's strong primary challenge to Hillary Clinton had already given new generations of workers and youth a display of what powerful bourgeois forces can and will do when they've decided the result of a nomination or election beforehand.

The ruling layers and top rungs of those who do their bidding live by different rules and moral standards. "Lyin'

Hillary" is wrong only in the many, many others that Trump's description lets off the hook, in both capitalist parties. Sanders and Trump alike decried the "rigged" system, whose game they themselves have contentedly played and profited from for years, and will continue to do so. But the eyes of millions of working people have been opened not to shadowy conspiracies, but to the everyday functioning of bourgeois politics in the United States and, in one form or another, the world over.

The former stability of the two-party shell game will not be restored.

◆

The Clintons' eight years in the White House, from 1993 to 2001, initiated the anti-working-class course that was continued over the subsequent two-term Republican and Democratic administrations of George W. Bush and Barack Obama. The record foreshadows what's in store for working people in coming years, whichever candidate wins.

The starkest example of this course was the Clinton administration's 1996 "welfare reform," which has slashed the percentage of families below the official US poverty line receiving government cash benefits from nearly 70 percent at that time to 23 percent in 2015. Hillary Clinton, who says "advocating for children and families has been the cause of my life," continues to this day to defend that cruel legislation.

The Clintons and their supporters promised jobs in place of welfare. But the jobs have trickled away, and the "safety net" is gone.

Former US senator Daniel Patrick Moynihan said twenty years ago that the Clinton administration would "go down in history as [the one] that abandoned, eagerly abandoned, the national commitment to dependent children." He couldn't have been more correct.

Health insurance rates under the Obama administration's *un*-Affordable Care Act will rocket between 30 and 60 percent in many states in 2017, and some 1.5 million working people will lose the plans they're currently covered by. Yet both Clinton and Trump continue to oppose government-funded universal health care. Trump says he will "repeal and replace Obamacare" altogether, thereby threatening to increase the 30 million plus people who have no medical coverage of any kind. Clinton promises vaguely to "fix what's broken." But it was the Clintons' own 1993 "Health Security Act," defeated in the Democratic-controlled Congress at the time, that cast the mold, holding workers' health care hostage to the profits of giant pharmaceutical corporations and increasingly interlocked insurance and hospital companies, as well as sharply rising charges for every aspect of medical attention.

The Clinton years were marked, among other things, by the largest jump in the federal and state prison population under any two-term president (up 60 percent between 1993 and 2001). Their administration presided over the highest annual number of deportations in US history (1.8 million). Legislation the Clinton White House supported and signed vastly expanded the number of federal crimes subject to capital punishment, whose use both Hillary Clinton and Donald Trump defend.

No one who watched the Clinton machine organize delegates at the 2016 Democratic convention to scream

"USA! USA!" in an attempt to silence delegates chanting "No more war!" would be surprised that it was the Clinton White House that coined the jingoistic description of the imperialist USA as "the indispensable nation." (Nor that the first Clinton administration spokesperson to broadcast that lie in the 1990s was its secretary of state Madeleine Albright, who during the 2016 primaries warned "there's a special place in hell" for women who don't support Hillary Clinton.)

Clinton has repeatedly called for a "no fly zone" over Syria, a policy that could only be enforced by a readiness to shoot down Moscow's warplanes, a direct military conflict with Russia. This stance is in line with her support for a quarter-century-long chain of US-initiated wars and military operations extending from Libya and Iraq, to Afghanistan and Pakistan. Including the Clintons' US-organized bombing campaigns and "special operations" in Iraq, Yugoslavia, and Somalia between 1993 and 2001, hundreds of thousands on all sides have already been killed or sustained life-crippling injuries as these conflicts spread. With further expansion in sight.

◆

It was during the Clintons' two terms in the White House that some of the harshest measures were taken to ratchet up the decades-long attempts by the US imperialist rulers to overturn Cuba's socialist revolution. That course also is enumerated in *The Clintons' Anti-Working-Class Record*.

With the passage of bills known as the Torricelli and Helms-Burton Acts, the latter signed into law by Clinton, Washington's brutal economic war against Cuban working people was intensified. This came as Cuba's decades-long trade relations with the USSR and Eastern Europe had disappeared overnight, and the Cuban Revolution faced—and surmounted—the greatest test yet in its history.

The Clinton administration turned a blind eye to provocations by Florida-based Cuban counterrevolutionaries who staged overflights of the island's airspace in hopes of prompting defensive action by Havana that could become a pretext for US retaliation, even military action. While Washington did nothing to halt these repeated assaults on Cuba's sovereignty, the Clintons' Justice Department framed up and railroaded to federal prison five Cuban revolutionaries living in Florida who were working for the Cuban government to prevent such provocations and violence against the Cuban people. Three of them were condemned to prison for life.

The US rulers fear the record of Cuba's socialist revolution for the same reason they fear the US working class. They sow lies and slanders about Cuba for the same reason they do about us. Above all, they fear the workers and farmers who made and defend Cuba's socialist revolution and its communist leadership *because of the example they've set*. The example that we *can* overcome the divisions they sow among us, that we *can* make a socialist revolution and establish a government that acts in our class interests. That we *can* extend active solidarity to struggles by working people the world over. That working people *can* and will transform ourselves and what we're capable of as we take power and transform society.

It's not just the *provision* of medical treatment that will change—to take one of the Cuban Revolution's best-known conquests. It's not just that everyone will have access to clinics, hospitals, and medicines. More importantly, as we uproot capitalism's dog-eat-dog social relations, the exploitation of one human being by another, those who will be trained under those transformed social relations will become different human beings. *That* is what will make the transformation of medical care possible.

And that example is what the US rulers fear most about the Cuban Revolution.

◈

During the 2016 US elections, the Socialist Workers Party has run a working-class campaign presenting Alyson Kennedy for president and Osborne Hart for vice president, as well as candidates for governor and the US Senate across the country, from California and Washington to New York and Florida. Unlike Hillary Clinton, Donald Trump, Bernie Sanders, and other capitalist candidates—all of whom address working people as *objects* of government policy, not *the makers* of revolutionary political change—the Socialist Workers Party candidates and their supporters have campaigned alongside fellow workers. They've done so in marches and actions against killer cops, on picket lines and other labor actions, and above all—day in and day out, region after region—on porches and doorsteps in working-class neighborhoods across the United States and Puerto Rico.

Campaigning in an undiscriminating way in the working class isn't something socialist workers do primarily when there's an election. It's what we do year round. We talk with other working people about a course of revolutionary struggle and join with them in demonstrations, strikes, political meetings, and other activities, small and large. We emphasize the self-destructive dead end of the reactionary politics of resentment. We discuss how our class can carry out a course of political action based on our class interests, not those of our capitalist employers, their government, and their parties, and why we need our own political party to do that. To all we say, our party is your party—if you agree, join with us to fight for this future.

One thing is startling by its breadth and depth: ever since the blows of the 2008–09 crash, there is growing openness among working people to talk and debate with each other about the broadest social and political questions facing our class, our unions, and our allies. Workers everywhere are looking for an explanation of capitalism's grinding and destructive decline, and, even more importantly, how to chart a way forward to combat its consequences.

That's why books such as *The Clintons' Anti-Working-Class Record* have an important place. As you read it, you will be struck time and again by the fact that the three articles it includes were published in earlier versions more than eight years ago in issue no. 14 of *New International* magazine. One piece is based on a talk presented by Jack Barnes more than fifteen years ago. But the words read as if spoken today!

The photos, illustrations, graphs, and other new information that have been incorporated update trends already evident since the 1990s.

The book is one of three titles published this election year by Pathfinder Press to help working people address the far-reaching political questions that we and others in the working class need answers to in order to fight more effectively and win. It stands alongside *Are They Rich Because They're Smart? Class, Privilege, and Learning Under Capitalism*, also by Jack Barnes, and *Is Socialist Revolution in the US Possible? A Necessary Debate Among Working People* by SWP leader Mary-Alice Waters. All three books build politically on another title by Barnes, *Malcolm X, Black Liberation, and the Road to Workers Power*, published in 2009 at the height of the paralyzing financial crisis.

In addition to translations into Spanish and French for use around the world, these books are right now being translated in Iran into the Farsi language. They will be distributed widely in bookshops and libraries there and well beyond Iran's borders. Their broad circulation demonstrates how the scope and explosiveness of the capitalist crisis, and the response of working people to its consequences, are truly worldwide.

◆

When the first modern communist organization was founded in 1847, the workers from Germany, Britain, and elsewhere who initiated it recruited two young revolutionaries named Karl Marx and Frederick Engels and asked them to help draft a founding program (what we know today as the Communist Manifesto), as well as a set of organizational rules they considered essential to a successful fight to realize that program. Second among the conditions of membership was "revolutionary energy and zeal in propaganda."

The aim of *The Clintons' Anti-Working-Class Record* and its two companion titles is to provide new political tools for workers who—amid today's mounting crises, and opportunities to build a working-class party—will read these books, share them door to door in workers districts, and use them in struggle, with just that kind of energy and zeal.

Steve Clark
OCTOBER 23, 2016

STEVE CLARK is a member of the National Committee of the Socialist Workers Party and editorial director of Pathfinder Press.

Part I
'Ending Welfare As We Know It'
(March 2001)

'Ending Welfare As We Know It'

(MARCH 2001)

THE CLINTONS ARE NOW, finally, out of the White House. From the outset of his 1992 presidential campaign, the Socialist Workers Party insisted that "Bill" Clinton would be a war president, a prison president, a death-penalty president. He would be a president, like those before him, whose course at home and abroad was aimed at serving the class interests of the US ruling families. Above all, we insisted that the Clintons had not been, and would not be, friends of the working class, in city or country.

The same we can say with confidence is true of Clinton's successor, George W. Bush, and of the Congress, then and now.

The landmark of the Clinton administration's anti-working-class assault, carried out in tandem with the Republican-controlled Congress, was contemptuously named the Personal Responsibility and Work Opportunity Reconciliation Act of 1996. This brutal, anti-working-class legislation eliminated Aid to Families with Dependent Children (AFDC), put a federally dictated lifetime limit of five years on welfare payments to any family, and allowed state governments to cap the number of years at an even lower level than five. States receiving federal "block grants" under the new Temporary Assistance for Needy Families (TANF) program are *not* required to spend those funds on cash payments to families—and more and more often they *don't*.

The "reform" was an incarnation of Clinton's reactionary 1992 campaign pledge to "end welfare as we know it," but it was also more than that. It was the biggest single success of the rulers so far in beginning to erode the federal Social Security system—a concession forced from the employing class in the 1930s as a by-product of massive working-class struggles that built the industrial unions and advanced the integration of Blacks into industrial jobs. Those conquests were widely expanded in the 1960s and 1970s, as the powerful proletarian-based Black rights movement and its broad social extensions wrested further weighty gains from the ruling class: Medicare, Medicaid, "SSI" (Supplemental Security Income) disability benefits, and cost-of-living protections.

Under the Clintons' "welfare reform," immigrants without "papers" were explicitly denied not only TANF benefits but also food stamps, Medicaid, and SSI payments. Even immigrants with "legal" residency (that is, a "Green Card") were barred from food stamps and federal disability protection. TANF and Medicaid "eligibility" was denied them for five years and then left up to state governments.[1]

---

1. As a result of growing dissatisfaction with these provisions of the "reform," federal legislation adopted in 2002 made immigrants under eighteen years of age with a Green Card eligible for food stamps, as it did adults who've had resident status for at least five years.

Clinton's welfare legislation—not just its basic provisions, but even its *name*—was taken over lock, stock, and barrel from a plank in the so-called Contract with America promised by the Newt Gingrich–led Republican majority that swept into Congress in 1994, two years after Clinton was elected.

The most vocal and historically clearest opponent in Congress of the anti-working-class destructiveness of the bipartisan "welfare reform" was Democratic senator Daniel Patrick Moynihan of New York. The legislation was "an act of unprecedented social vindictiveness," Moynihan said. Its consequences for children, women, and others might initially be buffered by the paper-fueled "tech-stock" bubble of the late 1990s, he said, but these effects would explode with a vengeance during the next inevitable deep recession—*like the one we're entering right now in 2001.*

"In a very little while as the time limits come into effect," Moynihan warned, "we will say, 'why are these children sleeping on grates?'"

Moynihan, a Harvard sociology professor for many years, had long been a critic of AFDC. On their own, Moynihan said, cash payments to dependent children, most of them in families headed by women, couldn't address what he considered the roots of poverty among African Americans: *joblessness.* Especially among young Black men, it was at "disaster levels." Without a federal public works program to tackle that crisis—and this was at the heart of what Moynihan recounted—poorer families in Black communities would continue to be torn apart. More and more of them would be headed by single women, with less and less assistance, unable to provide a stable economic and social haven of support for children.

Vivid descriptions of such devastation of families in working-class districts in nineteenth century England abound in *Capital* by Karl Marx and *The Condition of the Working Class in England in 1844* by Frederick Engels.

But so long as dog-eat-dog capitalist social relations exist, the family is what children, the elderly, the sick, and other working people have to fall back on.

In 1965, when Moynihan was a little-known assistant secretary of labor in the Lyndon Baines Johnson administration, he had written an internal report entitled *The Negro Family: The Case for National Action*. "The Negro American revolution is rightly regarded as the most important domestic event of the postwar period in the United States," he wrote. "Nothing like it has occurred since the upheavals of the 1930's which led to the organization of the great industrial unions." As a result of that struggle, he said, the expectations of Blacks "will go beyond civil rights," and "they will now expect that in the near future equal opportunities will produce roughly equal results."

Equality isn't possible, however, so long as "the racist virus in the American blood stream still afflicts us," Moynihan pointed out. It's not possible so long as the gap in income and living standards "between the Negro and most other groups in American society is widening."

Those conditions had been magnified by the rapid migration of Blacks from the rural South to segregated ghettos in northern cities that began during World War I. Moynihan himself had lived much of his childhood in New York's Hell's Kitchen in an Irish working-class family headed by his mother. Drawing on that experience, he wrote that—like the northward "Great Migration" of Blacks—it had been the abrupt transition from rural Ireland to large cities in the United States "that produced the wild Irish slums of the 19th Century Northeast."

"Eventually, the Irish closed that gap, and Moynihan has no doubt that the Negroes will too," said *Time* magazine in a 1967 cover story about him. But that's where the class limitations of Moynihan's bourgeois liberal outlook came into play. He didn't give enough weight to the fact that in addition to many common economic and social conditions bearing down on all working people, workers who are Black confront a unique, concrete historic obstacle to "closing the gap"—systematic discrimination, bigotry, and physical dangers simply due to the color of their skin.

That national oppression is something Irish and other workers who are Caucasian do not confront. Like Italians, Greeks, or many other immigrants, they became "white" over time in the racist US capitalist society (at least enough to "pass" as a national grouping). But descendants of African slaves do not—even those who "act white." They bear a lasting relic under capitalism of the barbaric slave trade and involuntary servitude. A relic, above all, of the bloody defeat of post–Civil War Radical Reconstruction and decades of legal Jim Crow racist segregation across the US South and de facto discrimination nationwide. It's a deeply entrenched legacy that only the overturn of the dictatorship of capital and revolutionary conquest of power by the working class can open the road to fighting to end for all time.

Not only did the Johnson administration reject the proposals in *The Negro Family: The Case for National Action,* but when Moynihan's 1965 report was leaked to the press, he was condemned by many liberals, Black nationalists, and middle class radicals as a racist who "blamed the victim," especially Black women. It's clear that most of these "critics" never bothered to read or seriously consider what Moynihan wrote.[2]

Nor did Moynihan convince Richard Nixon to take action on public works or other proposals when he served as White House urban affairs adviser in 1969, although Moynihan did get Nixon's ear more often than he had gotten LBJ's. A Family Assistance Plan proposed by Nixon with Moynihan's backing—a monthly "guaranteed minimum income" for a family of four, regardless of how many parents were in the home—was defeated by a Senate coalition of liberal Democrats and conservative Republicans. Nixon implemented the "Philadelphia Plan," for the first time setting affirmative-action targets for hiring Blacks on federally funded construction projects. And he ended the draft.

But the percentage of children living below the government's own poverty level kept climbing—from 14 percent in 1968 to 23 percent at the opening of the Clinton administration in 1993. So when Clinton publicly cited Moynihan's 1965 report in order to rationalize his pledge to "end welfare as we know it," Moynihan had had enough. The senior senator from New York shouted from the rooftops that Clinton's legislation promoted "cruelty" toward fami-

---

2. A half century later, a few liberals and especially nationalist-minded Blacks have acknowledged much of what Moynihan observed and recorded. These include Ta-Nehisi Coates, author of the 2015 best-seller *Between the World and Me*, written in response to the police killings of Eric Garner, Tamir Rice, and the "friskings, detainings, beatings, and humiliations . . . common to black people." In a 2013 *Atlantic* magazine article titled "Revisiting the Moynihan Report, Cont.," Coates said it's "really hard to separate out segregation from employment and family stability. That's a subject worthy of debate. But Moynihan didn't get debate. He got condemnation."

lies and perpetuated "social devastation." That Democratic administration was destined to "go down in history as [one] that abandoned, eagerly abandoned, the national commitment to dependent children."

Shortly before leaving office in January 2001, Clinton boasted that 8 million people nationwide had been slashed from state welfare rolls—a 60 percent drop in less than half a decade. What the bourgeois supporters of this legislation don't trumpet so loudly, however, is that the vast majority of these former AFDC recipients, if they've been able to find work at all, have been pressed into jobs at minimum wage *or below it,* with few if any health, pension, or vacation benefits.

And that has been during the *high point* of the upturn in the capitalist business cycle. As the first targets of the legislation's five-year limit are cut off permanently from welfare payments in the months ahead, they will find themselves in the midst of mounting layoffs and rising unemployment.

Clinton's 1996 act was the first time that an entire group of working people—single mothers and their children—has been eliminated from the kind of protections Social Security is supposed to offer to retirees, children, workers injured or thrown out of a job, and others vulnerable to the instabilities and devastations inherent in capitalism, both in good times and bad.

What's more, this section of the working class is one that's expanding in the United States. In 1965, when Moynihan wrote *The Negro Family,* the "crisis" figure he cited for the number of Black children raised in families headed by single women was 25 percent. A half century later, that's the percentage for *all single-parent households headed by women,* whatever their skin color. The figure for Blacks has

'Welfare reform'—
its toll on the working class

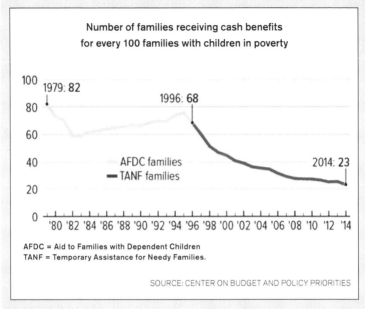

Number of families receiving cash benefits
for every 100 families with children in poverty

1979: 82

1996: 68

AFDC families
TANF families

2014: 23

'80 '82 '84 '86 '88 '90 '92 '94 '96 '98 '00 '02 '04 '06 '08 '10 '12 '14

AFDC = Aid to Families with Dependent Children
TANF = Temporary Assistance for Needy Families.

SOURCE: CENTER ON BUDGET AND POLICY PRIORITIES

Under the blows of the slow-burning depression signaled by the 2001 and 2008-09 recessions, the four million single mothers without jobs in 2014 (by government figures) was higher than the number unemployed when the Clinton-Gingrich so-called "workfare" reform was adopted. What's more, the percentage of women counted by the government as part of the labor force has been pushed down to 56.6 percent, the lowest since 1988.

Yet the proportion of families below the poverty line receiving benefits plunged from nearly 70 percent to 23 percent.

In addition, a third of state governments have adopted caps of lower than five years (e.g., two years in Kansas, only one in Arizona), and the buying power of benefits has been cut by at least a third, since the "reform" has no cost-of-living adjustment in states' block grants, which haven't increased since 1997!

risen to more than 70 percent.

Meanwhile, the poverty, lack of steady employment, and disintegration of families and other social relations— all imposed by the operations of capitalism on millions of working-class men, women, and children—register the inevitable consequences of a social system based on class exploitation and national oppression.

In this regard, another well-known article by Moynihan—a 1993 piece entitled, "Defining Deviancy Down"— poses questions that are important for the working-class vanguard. Moynihan wrote the article shortly after the spring 1992 social explosion in Los Angeles in reaction to the acquittal of four cops whose arrest and beating of Rodney King, an African American, had been widely televised.

Among the "deviant" social trends Moynihan focused on were the accelerating breakdown of the family structure, the sharp reduction in real income of poor families receiving AFDC benefits, and the rising violent crime rate (the last of these peaked the following year and has been falling since then). This was not the first time in American history, he said, that such "crime, violence, unrest, [and] lashing out at the whole social structure had been seen," especially among jobless "young men" from "broken families." Once again calling on his own working-class family background, Moynihan noted lessons "from the wild Irish slums of the 19th century Eastern seaboard to the riot-torn suburbs of Los Angeles."

The biggest danger, Moynihan said, is yielding to those social layers who "benefit from redefining the problem as essentially normal and doing little to reduce it"—"defining deviancy down," in his words. (Moynihan was speaking from his own class standpoint, about dangers to the capitalist government, political parties, and social order they represent.)

On the one hand, wrote Moynihan, "This redefining has evoked fierce resistance from defenders of 'old' standards, and accounts for much of the present 'cultural war' such as proclaimed by many at the 1992 Republican National Convention." He didn't elaborate on that reference, but he clearly had in mind the widely publicized convention speech in which Patrick Buchanan recounted (with considerable exaggeration) how US Army and National Guard units—"M-16s at the ready"—had taken back Los Angeles "block by block" that spring. In the same way, Buchanan said, "we must take back our cities and take back our culture and take back our country." That's how the "war going on in our country for the soul of America" will be won, Buchanan said. "It is a cultural war, as critical to the kind of nation we will one day be as was the Cold War itself."

On the other hand, Moynihan pointed to "solutions," also clearly not to his liking, that were gaining ground among more dominant sections of both ruling-class parties, including the recently elected Democratic administration of Bill and Hillary Clinton. "We are building new prisons at a prodigious rate," Moynihan cautioned at the close of his article. "Similarly, the executioner is back. There is something of a competition in Congress to think up new offenses for which the death penalty seems the only available deterrent."

That's why Moynihan, the liberal politician and professor, was opposed to "defining deviancy down." But for working people—for reasons of our own independent class interests—the stakes are much greater in not "defining down" social attitudes, habits, and conditions that divide our class, or that tear apart our political confidence, disciplined functioning, combativity, and morale.

Preying on fellow workers and farmers; judging each other on the basis of skin color, national origin, religion, or sex, instead of what we *do*; showing up drunk or stoned to a picket line or defense guard—none of this is "essentially normal" to a working class that is organizing and resisting, a class whose emancipation from exploitation can only be won by our own independent political organization and disciplined action. None exemplifies the norm included by Marx and Engels in the rules they drafted in 1847 for the world's first communist organization—"a way of life and activity which corresponds" to the political integrity and aims of the class-conscious workers movement.

That's the challenge that has faced every revolutionary movement of the working class and oppressed—from the mass workers struggles that forged the industrial unions in the United States; to the Black-led mobilizations for civil rights that brought down Jim Crow segregation and opened the road to internationalist working-class leaders such as Malcolm X; to the Rebel Army that led the workers and farmers of Cuba in a triumphant socialist revolution; to the struggle for a proletarian party that will make possible a socialist revolution in the United States.

Rulers' attacks on abortion rights

Over the quarter century since the Supreme Court's *Roe v. Wade* ruling, the political backlash from sections of the bourgeoisie against decriminalization of a woman's decision to end a pregnancy has been at the center of assaults on the social and economic gains of women. It is part of the broader attack on the rights and living conditions of working people.

Despite George W. Bush's election campaign rhetoric, the new administration is no more likely than its predecessors to attempt a head-on assault against a woman's right to choose. Nonetheless, attacks on abortion rights continue, and they've been made easier by the character and content of the 1973 court ruling.

Roe v. Wade was based not on a woman's right "to equal protection of the laws" guaranteed by the Fourteenth Amendment to the Constitution, but on medical criteria instead. During the first three months ("trimester"), the court ruled, the decision to terminate a pregnancy "must be left to the medical judgment of a pregnant woman's attending physician" (not to the woman herself, but to a doctor!).

At the same time, the court allowed state governments to ban most abortions after "viability," described in *Roe v. Wade* as the point at which a fetus is "potentially able to live outside the mother's womb"—something that medical advances inevitably make earlier and earlier in the pregnancy.

Opponents of women's rights have taken advantage of the Supreme Court's "medical" criteria from the outset. And they've made the most of the fact that the 1973 court decision was handed down while a raging debate had not yet been fought out and won by those who insisted that a woman's decision on this medical procedure falls under the protection of our hard-won constitutional rights.

The Fourteenth Amendment to the US Constitution, ratified in 1868, was a direct conquest of the Second American Revolution. Among its provisions, the amendment established that neither federal nor state authorities could "deny to any person within its jurisdiction the equal protection of the laws"—not to any *male* person, not to any person of a particular *race*, not just to any person who is a *citizen*. No government could deny those rights *to any person*—period. That's what the Fourteenth Amendment says.

Nonetheless, for more than a century, one federal court after another denied women just that. It wasn't until 1971 that the US Supreme Court—in an opinion written by Chief Justice Warren Burger, a Nixon appointee—finally affirmed that women were included in the Fourteenth Amendment's "equal protection under the laws."[3]

That shift, of course, didn't come as a sudden "judicial epiphany." It was the product of victories won in the streets in the 1950s and 1960s by millions of fighters for Black rights, as well as ongoing mobilizations against Washington's murderous war in Vietnam. Those battles, in turn, gave impetus to a new wave of activity and consciousness around the fight for women's rights.

But when the Supreme Court issued its opinion on abortion rights in 1973, the justices retreated. They rejected building on their ruling just two years earlier affirming women's equal protection under the laws. Instead, they issued *Roe v. Wade*, which—in the words of one former US solicitor general—read more "like a set of hospital rules and regulations."

Since then, state governments have loaded on more than seven hundred laws erecting obstacles to women exercising their constitutional right—age restrictions, "consent"

---

3. For the first time since ratification of the Fourteenth Amendment in 1868, the US Supreme Court in its 1971 *Reed v. Reed* decision struck down a state law on grounds that it violated the amendment's Equal Protection Clause by discriminating against women. The Idaho state law in dispute gave preference to men over women in appointment as administrators of estates.

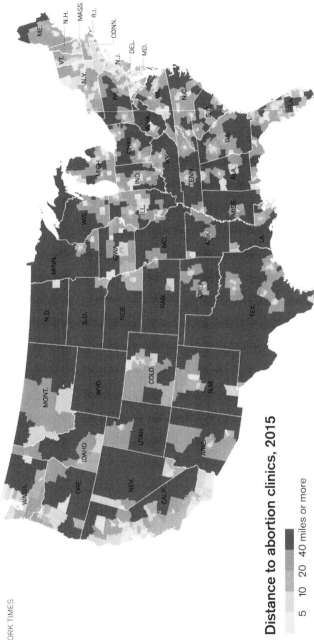

Distance to abortion clinics, 2015

5 10 20 40 miles or more

As opponents of women's rights imposed more and more onerous restrictions on access to abortion procedures, the average distance women must travel to reach a clinic has grown. In rural counties, more than three-quarters of women must drive more than 40 miles and one-third must drive more than 100 miles.

A victory in pushing back assaults on women's rights

Washington, DC, March 2016. Abortion rights supporters rally as Supreme Court heard challenge to restrictive Texas law, whose most burdensome provisions were struck down in June.

Since 2010, enemies of a woman's right to choose have increasingly focused on legislation requiring that abortions be treated differently from other out-patient surgical procedures. These assaults have been cynically packaged as "protections" of women's health.

On June 27, 2016, a major victory was registered pushing back "health" regulations restricting women's access to abortion. The US Supreme Court struck down provisions of a 2013 Texas law that had already resulted in closing half the state's forty abortion clinics, and if fully implemented could have reduced facilities to ten or fewer. Those consequences fell especially hard on women from the working class and from families on farms and in rural towns.

The court rejected the heart of the Texas legislation, which had (1) required any doctor performing abortions to have admitting privileges at a nearby hospital, and (2) demanded that family planning and prenatal clinics providing abortions meet hospital standards. Such requirements are not imposed on clinics handling more medically dangerous procedures, including colonoscopies, tonsillectomies, and dental surgery.

This victory for women's rights opens the way to fight to block similar anti-working-class legislation in Alabama, Mississippi, Wisconsin, and other states.

by parents, longer waiting periods, mandatory "counseling" about "alternatives," safety, and many more. Congress and the White House have barred (1) federal Medicaid funding for abortions, even those that are "medically necessary" (the 1976 "Hyde amendment"); (2) federal insurance coverage for abortions for women in the armed forces (except in cases of rape or incest, or danger to the woman's life), or use of military medical facilities for the procedure even if paid by other means; and (3) US government funding of "foreign aid" programs if abortion-related assistance is included in the program (the 1973 "Helms amendment").

These "restrictions" have taken a heavy toll. Among other things, today there is not a single medical facility providing abortions in a third of all cities and nearly 90 percent of the counties in the United States—*90 percent*! As a result, the extra cost of travel alone means that working-class women and those living in rural areas are at a big disadvantage in having access to this medical procedure.

Extending, defending universal suffrage

The Reconstruction Act of 1867, adopted by Congress over the veto of President Andrew Johnson, helped advance the fight for suffrage for Black males across the defeated

Confederacy by making it a precondition for readmission of states to the Union. The Fourteenth Amendment, ratified a year later, also contained provisions penalizing any state that denied the right to vote to freed slaves or other male US citizens under that state's jurisdiction.

Over the next decade, bloody battles to *defend* and *use* the franchise were organized and championed by the most politically advanced leaders of Radical Reconstruction governments in the states of the defeated slavocracy. But it took the political momentum of Radical Reconstruction to enfranchise Blacks in other states of the Union.

The Fifteenth Amendment to the Constitution—asserting that the right to vote shall not be denied or abridged by any federal or state government "on account of race, color, or previous condition of servitude"—was initially rejected by the legislatures in New York, New Jersey, Ohio, and California, among others. Finally ratified in 1870, that amendment and the struggle to win it gave an impulse, in turn, to extension of the franchise to women fifty years later, codified in the Nineteenth Amendment.

The US bourgeoisie, however, betrayed Radical Reconstruction at the close of the 1870s, and the broader workers and farmers movement was not yet strong enough to defend much less extend the conquests. In face of these setbacks, a nearly century-long reign of reactionary anti-Black terror was unleashed across the South, leading to the imposition in state after state of racist Jim Crow segregation—the model on which South Africa's infamous apartheid system was later based. Poll taxes, "literacy" tests, restrictions of every imaginable kind— and, above all, *lynchings and brutal beatings*—were used to terrify African Americans from going to the polls.

The counterrevolution had deadly consequences for tens

"Bloody battles to defend the right to vote were fought across the states of the defeated slavocracy. But it took the momentum of Radical Reconstruction to enfranchise Blacks elsewhere. The 15th Amendment, ratified in 1870, was initially rejected by legislatures in New York, Ohio, and California, among others."

Above: Popular US magazine depicts freed slaves voting for first time, November 1867. Federal Reconstruction Act adopted that year made suffrage for Black males a precondition for former Confederate states to rejoin Union.

Inset: May 19, 1870. Drawing of six-mile march in Baltimore, Maryland—largest of many held in US—celebrating passage of 15th Amendment, which barred federal and state governments from denying vote "on account of race, color, or previous condition of servitude."

of thousands of Chinese laborers in the US, too. Concentrated on the West Coast, they were targeted by pogroms and subject to numerous state laws restricting residency and employment, as well as legislation barring Chinese from entering the state. A federal Chinese Exclusion Act was adopted in 1882 and remained in effect until 1943, when it was repealed as part of sealing a wartime alliance against Japan with Nationalist Party (Kuomintang) forces in China.

By 1940 the cumulative consequences of the defeat of Radical Reconstruction had reached the point that only 3 percent of Blacks in the states of the old Confederacy were registered to vote. It took increasingly powerful protests and bloody battles in the streets and rural areas for more than a decade in the 1950s and 1960s to win back the franchise for Blacks— battles that broke down barriers not just in the South, but in many other localities across the United States, as well.[4]

Criminal injustice system

With majority support from both parties in Congress, Clinton signed legislation that expanded mandatory federal prison

---

4. Since 2010 more than twenty states have begun enforcing onerous restrictions on voting rights, targeting Blacks in particular. These include ID requirements, deadlines and other registration limits, and reductions in early voting. Attacks stepped up after a June 2013 Supreme Court decision struck down a key aspect of what African Americans had won with passage of the 1965 federal Voting Rights Act. The court gave state and local governments much greater leeway to change laws to restrict voting rights.

Under the impact of protests and vocal opposition, including in bourgeois political circles themselves, federal courts in 2016 rolled back restrictions in Texas, North Dakota, Wisconsin, and North Carolina. Challenges to similar voting-rights violations have been made in Alabama, Missouri, and Georgia, among other states.

sentences and increased their length, reduced protections against arbitrary search and seizure by cops and courts, increased property seizures *before* trials, and financed a record increase of more murderously armed cops on the streets. In the process, Clinton advocated and signed legislation expanding the number of federal crimes subject to capital punishment, laying justified claim to the shameful designation, the "death-penalty president."

Even before entering the White House, at the opening of the 1992 Democratic Party presidential race, the Clintons—Bill and Hillary arm in arm—took time off from stumping in the hotly contested New Hampshire primary to fly back to Arkansas, not to commute the death sentence of brain-damaged prisoner Ricky Ray Rector but to demonstratively preside over his grisly execution.

Not to be outdone by the Clintons' example, George Bush, while on the presidential campaign trail in 2000, followed in their footsteps. Over those months, the state of Texas, of which Bush was governor at the time, carried out the legal murder of the largest number of prisoners ever in any state in a single year in at least a century. Those forty were only a quarter of the executions carried out during Bush's six years in the statehouse.

During the eight years of the Clinton presidency, between 1993 and 2001, the number of people locked behind bars in US prisons jumped by nearly 60 percent. While the United States has 5 percent of the world's population, today it has 25 percent of the world's prisoners.

As throughout history, the overwhelming majority of those incarcerated are workers, with "the law" coming down disproportionately on those who are Black, Latino, or Native American. Today fully one of every three young

USA: World's top jailer . . .

The United States has the world's highest incarceration rate. As of 2015, some 1.5 million people are in federal or state prisons (see below); another 750,000 in local jails; and 4.8 million on parole or probation. Some 40 percent of those behind bars are Black.

The dark lines highlight the nearly 60 percent increase in the US prison population during the Clinton years alone.

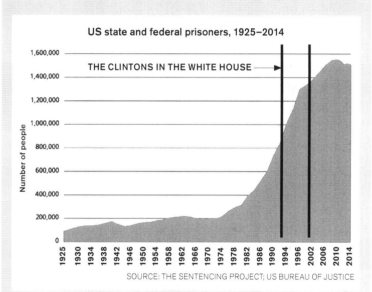

US state and federal prisoners, 1925–2014

SOURCE: THE SENTENCING PROJECT; US BUREAU OF JUSTICE

. . . and big-time executioner

Between 2007 and 2015, 365 people were executed in the United States. Hillary Clinton, the 2016 Democratic Party presidential candidate, continues to support use of this instrument of terror against working people, as do her Republican opponent, Donald Trump, and current President Barack Obama.

"The United States has 5 percent of the world population but 25 percent of the world's prisoners."

Above: Clinton signs "Violent Crime Control and Law Enforcement Act," September 1994. Law increased number of capital offenses to sixty; set mandatory federal prison sentences; expanded arbitrary searches; and authorized billions for more jails and cops.

Inset: Brain-damaged Ricky Ray Rector (left) was executed in Arkansas during 1992 presidential campaign. Bill Clinton, then governor, and Arkansas first lady Hillary Clinton returned from campaigning as show of support for execution.

males who are Black is either in prison, on parole, or on probation. Lockdowns and solitary confinement, with their dehumanizing effects—designed to make you feel helpless and worthless—are increasingly the norm.

The Clinton administration's 1994 Violent Crime Control and Law Enforcement Act accelerated the already rapidly expanding prison population in the United States. Among other provisions, the crime bill:

• Punished those convicted of possession of crack cocaine much more harshly than those found with powder cocaine, resulting in a disproportionate number of convictions and long sentences for African Americans (although they are no more likely to use or sell illegal drugs than others in the US population);

• Established mandatory minimum sentences, including a federal "three strikes" law requiring life imprisonment without parole for individuals with two prior convictions for drug trafficking or certain other felonies;

• Authorized prosecution as adults of defendants as young as thirteen charged with various crimes in which violence was used;

• Expanded the federal death penalty to some sixty offenses overall;

• Increased penalties for immigration-related offenses, including failure to obey a deportation order or reentry after being deported;

• Withdrew eligibility for federal college education grants from prisoners (followed in 1998 by two Clinton bills, one denying federal student loans to former prisoners convicted on drug charges; the second refusing federal housing assistance to or evicting families in which even one member has a "criminal record," even if not convicted); and

- Authorized federal funding to put more than one hundred thousand additional heavily armed cops on the streets of cities across the United States.

It's also necessary for class-conscious workers to recognize, explain, and raise our voices against the outrage that nowhere is the denial of the franchise to working people more far-reaching than in US prisons. Forty-eight out of the fifty states, as well as the federal government, bar prisoners sentenced on felony charges from voting while incarcerated (and many while on parole or probation). Twelve states disenfranchise certain people even *after* they're no longer behind bars or on parole or probation, in several cases *permanently*.[5]

No human being is 'illegal'

In 1996 Clinton signed into law the condescendingly named Illegal Immigration Reform and Immigrant Responsibility Act, adopted by a Republican Congress. That law expands the powers of the Immigration and Naturalization

---

5. This would be inexcusable even if only a handful of workers and others were denied voting rights in this way. But that's not the case. In 2016 nearly 6 million people—some 2.5 percent of the adult US population—have temporarily or forever lost the right to cast a ballot due to a felony conviction. In Alabama, Florida, Kentucky, Mississippi, Tennessee, and Virginia, more than 7 percent of the adult population was barred from voting on this basis in 2010. Nationwide nearly 8 percent of African American men are disenfranchised, with between 20 percent and 23 percent in Florida, Kentucky, and Virginia!

In August 2016 Virginia governor Terry McAuliffe restored voting rights by individual executive orders to 13,000 former prisoners, after the state Supreme Court earlier in the year overruled his blanket order returning the franchise to 206,000 former inmates. But the Virginia law permanently stripping the right to vote from those convicted on felony charges (unless lifted by the governor) remains in force.

Deportation, 'E-Verify,' and *la migra*

US OFFICE OF IMMIGRATION STATISTICS, AUGUST 2016

COURTESY AMERICAN IMMIGRATION COUNCIL

Immigrants to US without papers can be held—at times for more than a year—in freezing concrete cells without adequate bedding, food, water, medical care, showers, and toilets. **Above**: Douglas, Arizona, detention center, September 2015.

US immigration officials divide what most of us call "deportations" into two categories: "*removals*" (immigrants deported by judicial order and subject to felony charges if they re-enter); and "*returns*" (individuals turned back at the border or deported with no order).

Deportations overall reached an all-time high of more

than 1.8 million in 2000, the last year the Clintons were in the White House, and fell to under 600,000 in 2014. The biggest reason for the decline is that fewer people have been immigrating to the United States, due to the capitalist economic crisis. In fact, as a result of high US jobless levels, more Mexicans living in the United States have *returned* to Mexico since 2009 than have immigrated north of the border.

"Removal" orders rose to new highs during the first five years of the Obama administration. More foreign-born workers lost jobs and were forced out of the US as a result of "E-Verify" audits of Social Security numbers than in the hated *la migra* factory raids of the Clinton and Bush years. Those raids became counterproductive to the US rulers in the wake of millions-strong demonstrations in 2006–07 by immigrants and their supporters and widespread protests by working people against workplace assaults by SWAT-style immigration cops.

The average daily population of immigrant men, women, and children held in some 200 miserable detention prisons across the US mounted from under 8,000 a day in 1996 to 34,000 in 2014.

Service (INS)[6] to round up and deport those charged with being "illegal" immigrants without the right to judicial review or appeal. Simultaneously the White House and Congress funded the expansion of the hated *la migra* into

---

6. In March 2003, as part of a post–9/11 reorganization of federal police and spying agencies, the state functions carried out by the INS were transferred from the Department of Justice to the newly formed Department of Homeland Security and divided among three bodies: US Immigration and Customs Enforcement (ICE); US Customs and Border Protection (CBP); and US Citizenship and Immigration Services (USCIS).

the largest federal cop agency, one that has stepped up factory raids and deportations to record numbers in recent years.

Far from aiming to stem the flow of labor from the Americas and elsewhere into the United States, the rulers need immigrant workers as a superexploitable labor pool and intend for their repressive measures to heighten insecurity and fear among them. Maintaining this second-class status for immigrants is one of the ways the employers promote competition and conflict among workers in order to press down wages and conditions of the entire working class and further divide and weaken the unions and efforts to organize the unorganized.

Under the Star Chamber provisions of the 1996 Anti-Terrorism and Effective Death Penalty Act (once again, the name itself stands in condemnation of its ruling-class authors), the US government has stepped up its "preventive detention" of individuals on the basis of "secret evidence." Most are immigrants from Arab or other majority Muslim countries accused of links with "terrorist organizations"—the code word the US rulers increasingly use to rationalize both assaults on democratic rights at home and military strikes abroad (actually mass murder from the air).

The Anti-Terrorism and Effective Death Penalty Act also greatly weakens centuries-old habeas corpus protections, making it much easier for federal judges all the way up to the Supreme Court to deny the release or refuse to commute the death sentences of prisoners presenting evidence they were erroneously incarcerated or wrongly condemned to death. Among other things, the law denies the right of death-row prisoners to submit more than one habeas corpus petition for federal court review of their cases—"*one strike*" and you're out.

As a result of this legislation, together with the Illegal Immigrant Reform and Immigrant Responsibility Act, the number of immigrants held in US immigration jails any given day awaiting the outcome of threatened deportations has jumped to some 20,000 people at the opening of the new century—a 245 percent increase just since 1996.

A war president, too

During the days prior to Clinton's inauguration in January 1993, the outgoing Republican Bush administration rained down bombs on Iraq, as it had continued doing over the nearly two years since the "cease-fire" in the 1991 US-led Gulf War. The new Democratic administration followed suit the very next week. In fact, Iraqi civilians have been killed in intermittent US raids month in and month out since the 1991 war, and more have been wounded, many mutilated for life.

Washington's military campaign against the Iraqi people should remind us of something in Cuban General José Ramón Fernández's testimony in July 1999 before the Provincial People's Court of the City of Havana. The court was hearing a lawsuit filed by eight Cuban organizations to demand that the US government pay damages for the thousands of deaths and billions of dollars in physical destruction caused by Washington's decades-long efforts to overthrow the Cuban Revolution by force and violence.

The Cuban general reported that during the April 1961 US government-organized mercenary invasion of Cuba at the Bay of Pigs, Washington supplied the mercenaries with napalm, which they used against Cuban working people in the militia, armed forces, and police defending Cuba's sovereignty and territorial integrity, its socialist revolution. The one thousand five hundred invaders were defeated in fewer than seventy-two hours of combat during what Cubans call the battle of Playa Girón.

Citing a published account by one of the mercenary pilots, Fernández said the invaders' planes carried three tons of napalm bombs, which spray an incendiary jelly that clings to the flesh of human beings, burning and asphyxiating them. He reminded the Havana court that international rules of war signed by governments the world over (including by Washington) forbid the use of "weapons, projectiles, and materials designed to cause that kind of harm contrary to the normal laws of humanity. But those were precisely the type of bombs used by the armed forces of the United States."[7]

To the degree many of us know about the US rulers' use of napalm, we often associate it exclusively with the monstrous suffering inflicted by Washington and its allies on tens of thousands of human beings during the Vietnam War. But napalm had also been used extensively by US imperialism against the Japanese in the Pacific, and during Washington's barbaric razing to the ground of northern Korea a few years later. It was used by French imperialism during its unsuccessful wars to crush the Algerian and Vietnamese independence struggles, too.

We can point to many other examples of these atrocity-studded bipartisan war policies.

---

7. Brigadier General José Ramón Fernández's July 1999 testimony is available in *Playa Girón/Bay of Pigs: Washington's First Military Defeat in the Americas* (Pathfinder, 2001).

Even though Bush may not quite match the record of Clinton, who was the most antagonistic president to a Palestinian homeland in half a century, the new administration nonetheless will continue the course of its predecessor in supporting Tel Aviv's denial of the Palestinians' national rights and its bloody assaults and collective punishment of Arab youth and working people fighting for that goal.

The Clinton administration also led the efforts of the US and European imperialist rulers to restore capitalist social relations in Russia and other former republics of the Soviet Union, as well as across Eastern and Central Europe. These were the heydays of Washington's so-called "shock therapy" privatization in these countries, with shattering effects on the lives of millions of workers and farmers and the sudden enrichment of a privileged handful (including some Harvard professors and other US "economic advisers," "investors," and "entrepreneurs," who ended up as wealthy as the thieves they are).

Washington presided over the systematic destruction of the Yugoslav Revolution's conquest of national unification by breaking up that country along centuries-old national and religious divisions. In 1994–95 and again in 1999, the US rulers and their NATO partners employed cruise missiles and aerial bombardment from afar against working people in Serbia, Bosnia, Kosova, and elsewhere in the former Yugoslavia.

In the process, Washington reinforced US imperialism's post–World War II position as the dominant "European" military power.

Under Clinton the expansion of NATO extended the reach of US imperialism's armed might closer and closer to the borders of Russia, bringing in three former Warsaw

NATO expansion and US missile provocations

Twelve eastern and central European countries have been incorporated into the NATO imperialist military alliance since 1991. These are the three Baltic states directly bordering Russia—Estonia, Latvia, and Lithuania—as well as Albania, Bulgaria, Croatia, the Czech Republic, Hungary, Poland, Romania, Slovakia, and Slovenia.

With Moscow brutally annexing Crimea in 2014 and maintaining military pressure on the Ukraine/Russia border, a July

2016 NATO summit provocatively violated a 1997 NATO agreement with Russia "on Mutual Relations, Cooperation and Security."

Washington and other NATO members pledged that the alliance would "carry out its collective defence and other missions" by means other than "additional permanent stationing of substantial combat forces" near Russia's borders. To rationalize getting around this pact, the July 2016 summit announced that NATO will permanently "rotate" up to 4,000 US, German, UK, and Canadian troops through eastern Poland and the Baltic states.

In June 2002 the Bush administration withdrew from the 1972 Anti-Ballistic Missile Treaty with Moscow. The White House implemented plans for ground-based ABM systems in eastern Europe, Alaska, and California, as well as sea- and land-based systems in Asia.

The Obama administration deployed a ground-based antiballistic missile system in Romania in 2016, with another set for Poland in 2018. An ABM system targeting North Korea, China, and Russia, will be operational in South Korea in 2017.

None of these ABM systems come anywhere close to giving Washington the capacity to cripple long-range Intercontinental Ballistic Missiles from Russia or China in their boost or later stages, and thus none give the US rulers nuclear first-strike capacity. What's more, there's no reason to believe that's a reachable goal at any foreseeable time—for political reasons, above all.

Pact countries: the Czech Republic, Hungary, and Poland. During the 2000 presidential campaign both Bush and his Democratic opponent Albert Gore advocated further expansion, with the next countries in line—the former Soviet Baltic republics, Lithuania, Latvia, and Estonia (all of them militarily annexed under Stalin's direction in 1940)—bringing imperialist US military pressure ever nearer Russia's main urban centers.

The Clinton White House has already initiated plans for an Alaska-based anti-ballistic missile (ABM) system that will serve as the starting point for more extensive ground- and submarine-based missiles by the new Bush administration. The aim, with bipartisan backing in Congress, is to leverage US military might to increase the US rulers' political dominance vis-à-vis other powers in Europe that have developed nuclear arsenals: not only Paris and London, but Moscow first and foremost.

More immediately, a US anti-ballistic missile system will target China and North Korea, two countries in Asia where the imperialist yoke was thrown off half a century ago. Washington already has hundreds of nuclear-tipped missiles targeted on these two countries. In the process, the US rulers are slowly but surely drawing Tokyo into the world of nuclear weapons and delivery systems.

In addition, the US rulers seek to instill terror into the government of any semicolonial country—Iraq, Iran, India, Pakistan—that has built missile-based defenses that could be used against future imperialist aggression.

Defending Cuba's socialist revolution

This meeting today celebrates the fortieth anniversary of the April 19, 1961, victory of the Cuban defenders at Playa Girón over the mercenary invasion force organized and financed by the US government. Throughout these four decades, there has been overwhelming bipartisan support for Washington's unrelenting economic, political, and military aggression against the Cuban Revolution.

In October 2000, during his final months in office, Clinton signed an agricultural appropriations bill that—in ad-

"Washington presided over the systematic destruction of the Yugoslav Revolution's conquest of national unification by breaking up that country along centuries-old national and religious divisions."

"**US rulers and their NATO partners used cruise missiles and aerial bombardment from afar against working people in Serbia, Bosnia, and Kosova in the former Yugoslavia.**"

Above: Aleksinac, Yugoslavia. Coal mining town bombed by US and NATO forces, April 5, 1999. Raids destroyed a working-class neighborhood, killing 17 civilians and wounding more than 40.

Inset: Sarajevo, Yugoslavia, hospital, July 1992. Nurse at right lost her leg when Belgrade-backed Serbian forces in Bosnia shelled breadline.

dition to once again lining the pockets of agribusiness and capitalist farmers at the expense of working farmers and farm workers—contained a rider making long-standing administrative restrictions on travel to Cuba federal law. Now US residents who visit Cuba face criminal, in addition to civil, penalties.

Among other acts of hostility to the Cuban Revolution during his eight years—acts too numerous to review—Clinton in 1996 signed into law the so-called Cuban Liberty and Democratic Solidarity (Libertad) Act, also known as the Helms-Burton Law, which intensified the US economic war on Cuba. Four years earlier, as the Democratic candidate for president in 1992, he led the charge in championing another reinforcement of Washington's economic war against Cuba, the so-called Cuban Democracy Act or Torricelli Act, which George Bush senior, the still-serving Republican president, then signed.

In one of the most demonstrative attacks on the Cuban people and their revolution, the Clintons' White House framed up and railroaded to federal prison five Cuban revolutionaries living in south Florida—Gerardo Hernández, Ramón Labañino, Antonio Guerrero, Fernando González, and René González.

In predawn FBI raids in September 1998, the five were arrested and accused of being part of a "Cuban spy network" in Florida. After seventeen months of isolation in "the hole" at Miami's Federal Detention Center, in November 2000 "the Cuban Five"—as they've become known— went on trial for charges including conspiracy to commit espionage and, in the case of Gerardo Hernández, conspiracy to commit murder. Contrary to these frame-up charges, the five revolutionaries were in fact keeping the Cuban gov-

Victory in worldwide fight to free the Cuban 5

ESTUDIOS REVOLUCIÓN

RODOLFO BLANCO / AIN

Above: Cuban president Raúl Castro (in uniform) with (from left) Fernando González, Ramón Labañino, Gerardo Hernández, Antonio Guerrero, René González.

Inset: Celebrating victory, Camagüey, Cuba.

In June 2001 each of the five Cuban revolutionaries was convicted on all counts against them, including, in the case of Gerardo Hernández, "conspiracy to commit murder." The five were given sentences ranging from fifteen years to double life plus fifteen years. In 2013 and early 2014, Fernando

González and René González had served out their terms in full and returned to Cuba.

Through efforts by the Cuban government and a broadly supported international defense campaign, on December 17, 2014, Hernández, Ramón Labañino, and Antonio Guerrero—the three who remained behind bars on US soil—won their freedom. Washington commuted their sentences, and millions of Cubans poured into the streets to welcome them.

That same day, Cuban president Raúl Castro and US president Barack Obama announced that diplomatic relations between Cuba and the United States, broken by the US rulers in 1961, would be reestablished. Despite Obama's acknowledgment that decades of attempted economic strangulation of Cuba had failed to achieve the US aim of overturning the socialist revolution—and that it was time to try "something different"—Washington's brutal embargo remains intact and the US government still occupies territory and Cuba's best harbor at Guantánamo in the island's easternmost region, the cradle of Cuba's three revolutions in the nineteenth and twentieth centuries.

ernment informed about counterrevolutionary groups in the United States planning terrorist attacks against Cuba and against defenders of the Cuban Revolution in the US, Puerto Rico, and elsewhere.

Last year, in April 2000, the Clinton administration cynically exploited its half-year-long refusal to return six-year-old Elián González to Cuba—his country of birth, and home of his father, grandparents, and other close family members—in order to burnish the image of the INS and establish legal precedents reinforcing the agency's repressive powers. The predawn raid by heavily armed commandos of *la migra* to take the child from a home in Miami not only bolstered the powers of the Border Patrol—powers that are used day in and day out against the working class—but dealt a blow to the Fourth Amendment rights of all US residents to be safe in their homes from arbitrary searches and seizures.

The Bush administration, in both word and deed, is now carrying out its own campaign pledge to continue along this decades-long course of striving, by one means or another, to overturn Cuba's socialist revolution.

'Czar' for spying, home and abroad

During his closing days in office, Clinton issued a presidential directive establishing the post of "counterintelligence czar"—formally, the National Counterintelligence Executive—and Bush just this week made an appointment to this new top-level spy position.

According to press accounts, the post is "designed to facilitate a level of cooperation never seen before among the FBI, the CIA and the Pentagon, and will, for the first time, engage the rest of the government and the private sector as well." *The private sector as well?* What "private sector" police agencies are included? What strikebreaking rent-a-cops will now have more federal cover and encouragement? What snooping employers of all kinds?

One reporter for the big-business press covering the new position wrote that it will force "the American public to rethink long-accepted notions about what constitutes national security and the once-clear boundaries between domestic law enforcement, foreign intelligence gathering and defense preparedness."

In short, the counterintelligence czar will draw together Washington's "anti-terrorist" operations from Iran, Korea, and Somalia, to the immigrant family living down the

Fourth Amendment under fire

In the wake of the 9/11 attacks, the Bush and Obama administrations and Congress extended the encroachments on political rights by the Clinton White House. In early 2005 the National Counterintelligence Executive was made subordinate to an even more powerful "intelligence czar," the newly established Director of National Intelligence. The DNI is responsible to the president for the oversight and integration of operations by seventeen federal spying and cop agencies, from the CIA and FBI to branches of the US armed forces and beyond.

Washington has expanded phone, email, and Internet interception; the tracking of domestic and international financial transactions; monitoring of passenger lists of airlines and other transportation; and spying on political groups and individuals organizing opposition to Washington's policies. These measures were initially enacted as part of the Patriot Act, adopted in 2001 with only one "no" vote in the Senate and sixty-six in the House of Representatives and renewed in 2011. They were then incorporated, with a few cosmetic changes, in the USA Freedom Act, adopted by a bipartisan coalition in Congress and signed by Obama in 2015.

block. It will draw together the US rulers' "war on drugs" from the new US military bases in Colombia and Ecuador to working-class neighborhoods and factory locker rooms across North America. It will centralize the US government's informers, wiretapping, postal mail "covers," e-mail hacking, and plain old neighborhood snoops and tattlers. It will concentrate secret police operations against both "enemies" abroad and the labor movement and social protest organizations at home.

Whether the charge be "endangering national security" or "giving away business secrets," the US rulers will work to find a frame-up that sticks.

I raise the Clinton and Bush administrations' new counterintelligence czar not because there is reason to anticipate some tidal wave of repression around the corner. But the US rulers are already shifting gears from the last decade. They know they will face more and bigger battles as international capitalist competition drives them to slash wages, extend the workday, intensify speedup, cut Social Security protections, and further cripple the unions—around the world. And they are preparing to defend their class interests.

Part II
Roots of the 2008 World Financial Crisis
(May 2008)

Roots of the 2008 World Financial Crisis

(MAY 2008)

IT HAS NOW BEEN seven years since the Clintons vacated the White House. To hear tell from Hillary Clinton, Barack Obama, and the former president himself, almost all today's ills—from the ongoing war in Iraq, to declining real wages and employment for working people, to high finance's orgy of destruction, and more—can be laid at the foot of George W. Bush and the Republican Party.

In the Democratic primary electioneering, "Bill" Clinton has taken to modestly describing the years he and Hillary presided over the White House from 1993–2001 as "the eight best years we've had in modern history." (Yes, "*we*.")

Currents in the workers movement such as the Communist Party USA, like most other middle-class radicals and self-described socialists, insistently peddle this same "Bush-is-the-problem" story. All of them would have us believe that the policies carried out since Clinton left office in 2001, at home and abroad, were cooked up from scratch by the Republicans.

In trying to make this case stick, the Democrats and their advocates count on the greed of the bourgeois "outs" to once again become the "ins," a cycle that's been part of the capitalist two-party game for well over a century. They also count on shortness of memory. But it's not only class-conscious workers whose historical attention span is longer than that.

The most important elements of both domestic and foreign policy widely attributed today to the Bush administration originated during the years when the Clintons were "renting out" the Lincoln Bedroom.* At the time when Robert Rubin was Treasury Secretary, followed by Lawrence Summers. And Newt Gingrich was the Republican Speaker of the House of Representatives.

Imperialism and war

A "war on terrorism" began well before 9/11. Following the collapse of the Stalinist bureaucratic regime in the Soviet Union in 1991 and disintegration of the Warsaw Pact, the Clinton administration laid the foundations for the imperialist bourgeoisie's efforts to "transform," restructure, and strengthen its military posture, both at home and abroad. Initial steps included the passage of new laws that erode

---

* Between 1993 and 1996, more than 800 White House "guests"—invited by the Clintons to spend the night in the historic Lincoln Bedroom—donated at least $5.2 million to the Democratic National Committee. These included wealthy corporate CEOs and financiers of all kinds, as well as celebrities such as Steven Spielberg and Barbra Streisand.

When this high-level hustle of auctioning political access to the White House came to light in 1997, President Clinton defended the practice by saying, "They were my friends, and I was proud to have them here. And I do not believe people who lawfully raise money for people running for office are bad people. I think they are good people. They make the system work that we have now." *You can say that again!*

World capitalism's slow-burning depression

Average annual per capita GDP growth

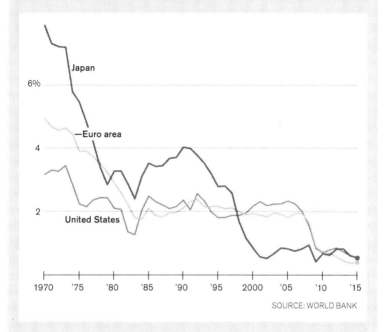

Japan

6%

—Euro area

4

2

United States

1970 '75 '80 '85 '90 '95 2000 '05 '10 '15

SOURCE: WORLD BANK

In 2016 most working people would laugh in derision and disgust at a presidential claim about "the eight best years we've had in modern history." But that hasn't stopped Barack Obama or Hillary Clinton from saying preposterous things like the economy is "pretty darn great right now" (Obama, March 2016), or "our economy is so much stronger" since Obama was elected (Clinton at the July 2016 Democratic convention).

The facts tell a different story. Since 2006, US economic growth per person (that is, the yearly change in what the government calls Gross Domestic Product, or GDP) has fallen sharply from the nearly 4 percent averaged over the previous fifty years. The per capita growth rate since 2006 has averaged less than 0.5 percent—yes, *less than half a percent per person per year.* And US capitalism is doing better than most of its imperialist rivals in Europe and in the Pacific and Asia.

Moreover, real gross domestic investment in capacity-expanding plant, equipment, and hiring has contracted since before the 2008–09 crisis, as has spending on roads, mass transportation, and other infrastructure by local, state, and federal governments.

the constitutional rights of working people in the United States—from detention based on "secret evidence," to deportation without judicial review and appeal.

The ongoing US-organized wars in Afghanistan (launched in September 2001) and Iraq (in March 2003) have both lasted longer than Washington's bloody engagement in World War II. And they are far from over, and far from being contained to their original arenas.

All three 2008 presidential candidates—John McCain, who has already clinched the Republican nomination, and the two Democratic primary survivors, Hillary Clinton and Barack Obama—say the US government should commit more troops to Afghanistan, and should have done so long ago. McCain, narrowing the opinion-poll gap with Obama and Clinton, is staking much of his campaign on presenting himself as the candidate whose vigorous support for the "surge" in Iraq and its extension to Afghanistan offers the best chance of bringing the largest numbers of US troops home the fastest.

Not a single one of these capitalist candidates supports the only course that is in the interests of working people in the United States and the world over: immediate and unconditional withdrawal of all US troops from both Iraq and

Afghanistan, as well as everywhere else US forces are deployed abroad. Only the Socialist Workers Party—and our 2008 ticket of Róger Calero for president, and his running mate Alyson Kennedy—are campaigning for that.

Grooming a 'new' Democrat

Prior to Clinton's election to the presidency in 1992, dominant sectors of the US ruling class had molded him to lead Democratic Party liberals rightward, to the "center."

Since the mid-1970s, when capitalism was hit with its first worldwide recession since World War II, the employing class has had diminishing room for substantial economic and social concessions to working people. Clinton's job was to distance the Democratic Party from the "New Deal"–style social welfare programs many workers identified with that party. It had claimed credit for them ever since rising labor battles in the 1930s wrenched concessions from Franklin D. Roosevelt's administration during the Great Depression. From the New Deal through Lyndon Johnson's "Great Society" in the mid-1960s, those programs had been the glue that held together the diverse Democratic Party coalition.

While draping itself in the Democrats' "progressive" mantle, the Clinton administration set out to change the party's complexion to such a degree that what had previously been its "moderate center" would become its broad majority and redefine what a liberal Democrat is. His apprenticeship included officiating twelve years as governor of Arkansas, as well as chairing the National Governors Association in 1986–87 and then, in 1991, the Democratic Leadership Council (DLC), which had been founded six years earlier to help push the party in that direction.

"Not a single capitalist candidate supports the only course that is in the interests of working people the world over: immediate and unconditional withdrawal everywhere US troops are deployed abroad."

Above: Dan Fein (center), Socialist Workers Party candidate for mayor of New York, at rally in Washington, DC, March 2009, to protest US-led wars in Iraq and Afghanistan.

Inset: Mary Martin (with bullhorn), Socialist Workers Party candidate for governor of Washington, at rally in defense of Kurds' fight for freedom, Seattle, August 2015.

Two years into Clinton's presidency, in November 1994, a Republican majority was elected in the House of Representatives, and a bipartisan convergence quickened. In 1996 alone "welfare as we know it" was wiped off the books; the "Anti-Terrorism and Effective Death Penalty Act" was adopted; and the "Immigration Reform and Immigrant Responsibility Act" was enacted, the biggest assault on the rights of the foreign-born since the end of World War II.

The Clinton administration also accelerated steps by the US rulers to try to counteract the declining rate of profit and the employers' "inadequate" returns on capital expenditures. The goal was to "encourage" the capitalists to expand industrial plant and equipment and employ growing numbers of workers in production. To that end, the administration and Congress adopted legislation that, along with other White House measures, helped the employing class erect the enormous edifice of household, real estate, corporate, and government debt, and its accompanying array of derivatives, that began to unravel with the first signs of a world financial crisis in 2007 and its acceleration early this year.

Nobody knows, nor can know, how this financial crisis will unfold. But it's not the result of "mistaken policies." It is a product of the workings of the laws of capitalism itself. It's a consequence, not a cause, of finance capital's development. The propertied US families have no choice but to engage in their debt-propelled course.

Just a month or so ago, in March 2008, the New York Federal Reserve Bank had to ante up $30 billion to undergird potential losses by bondholders of the failing Bear Stearns investment house, the fifth largest in the US before it went under. And the Fed's actions in financing JPMorgan Chase's buyout of Bear Stearns at bargain-basement prices signaled to finance capital that the US government would assume massive "private" risks in order to prevent a spiraling debt collapse.

It's simply a fact, not a prophecy, that in May 2008, millions of "homeowners" are now facing sharp hikes in interest payments on risky adjustable-rate mortgages in the United States—a swelling wave that will roll on for several years and drag in its wake more loan defaults and foreclosures. There will be bigger write-offs of losses by banks, hedge funds, insurance companies, and other holders of mortgage debt and derivative contracts.

Countless bourgeois politicians and financial commentators have sought to pin the blame for the mounting "mortgage crisis" on former Federal Reserve Board chairman Alan Greenspan. In happier days, many of them sang his praises—some even crowned him "the maestro"—for his twenty years of service to four presidents, Republican and Democratic, from his appointment by Reagan in 1987 through his departure from the Fed in early 2006, when George W. Bush was in office. Greenspan's latter-day detractors point to speeches he made in 2004 and 2005 extolling the "innovation [that] has brought about a multitude of new products, such as subprime loans," which have made it possible for "once more-marginal applicants"—a bourgeois euphemism for working-class families with low incomes—to buy homes. (And to lose them as they're unable to keep up the payments and fall deeper and deeper in debt.)

Greenspan has pricked the pretensions of these critics, however, by pointing to their class shortsightedness. In his 2007 memoir *The Age of Turbulence*, Greenspan makes no apologies. Whatever slips he may have made about a par-

Bank 'bailouts' and unicorns

The banking collapse continued throughout 2008, with the collapse of Lehman Brothers investment bank, as well as government-backed bailouts of failing banks and brokerages, insurance giants, finance and leasing companies, and manufacturers such as General Motors and Chrysler. *Forbes* magazine estimates the total price tag of federal bailouts at $16 trillion.

To stem the spiral, in early 2009 the FASB (Financial Accounting Standards Board)—the "private" capitalist body that sets accounting rules in the US—acted at the bipartisan urging of politicians in Washington to consecrate cooking the books. The FASB ruled that financial institutions no longer had to place a dollar value on risky or failing "assets" that reflected the amount for which they could be bought or sold on the market.

In place of this so-called mark-to-market accounting, the FASB now allowed "significant judgment" by banks, mortgage companies, and other financial institutions on the verge of insolvency (as well as others that weren't). They could "estimate" the value of their own "assets"—and thus of their losses.

Officially referred to as mark-to-model accounting, this quickly became known as mark-to-unicorn accounting. Through such magic, to cite just one example, in 2012 and 2013 Bank of America was able to "disappear" some $7.6 billion in cumulative losses and report a net income of $4 billion.

If only indebted workers and farmers could get some of those unicorns!

ticular kind of mortgage, he says, it was "worth the risk" in order to boost home ownership. The "protection of property rights, so critical to a market economy"—that is, to the lords of capital—Greenspan emphasizes, "requires a critical mass of owners to sustain political support." To those who now rebuke him, the former Fed chief is saying: What plan do you have to try to persuade workers that they, too, are "property holders" with a stake in preserving the capitalist system?

But Greenspan alone was not, and could not have been, responsible for the near-maniacal expansion of mortgage debt in the United States, nor its inevitable bust. He did not bring on deflating housing prices and spiraling mortgage crises in the United Kingdom, Ireland, Spain, and elsewhere. No runaway Federal Reserve chairman—supposedly acting contrary to the course and interests of the class he serves—is responsible for capitalist debt excess.

Quite the opposite. During at least the last half of Greenspan's tenure, investment banks such as JPMorgan Chase, Goldman Sachs, and others were entering into increasingly complex derivative transactions using leverage in the range of thirty-to-one (that is, $30 of payment obligations borrowed for every $1 of their own holdings). And so-called hedge funds, private equity firms, foreign currency traders, food commodity futures hoarders, and other dealers in what Karl Marx explained was "fictitious capital" were doing the same, often leveraged fifty- or even a hundred-to-one!

By the end of 2007, the outstanding value worldwide for such derivatives reached the previously unimaginable total of $596 trillion. In 2007 alone the single most "popular" variety of these massively leveraged bets actually doubled—so-called credit-default swaps, a form of supposed "insurance" against nonpayment of these same very risky deals. But as the direction of financial markets shifted at an accelerating pace in late 2007, the antidote became the poison.

Over the two decades since the 1987 stock market crash struck terror in the US rulers' hearts, they have maneuvered to avert a deep economic slump. As they've sought to hold down prices and interest rates, while at the same time spending billions on wars from Iraq to Yugoslavia to Afghanistan, their mounting debt has increasingly been bankrolled by governments and wealthy individuals around the world. Excluding Treasury bonds held by the Federal Reserve bank, more than half of these bonds—the US government's major credit instrument—are now, for the first time in history, held by these foreign entities.

The capitalists in China, who increasingly dominate the regime there, have been especially eager lenders to Washington and Wall Street. As of December 2007 they had bought up nearly $500 billion in US Treasury bonds— more than 20 percent of all such certificates outstanding worldwide, within a few months surpassing Japan as the number-one holder.

The Beijing regime's policy is to help keep the US dollar strong and maintain a competitive edge for Chinese manufactured goods in world markets. They are trading away improvements in the wages, social welfare, and living conditions of hundreds of millions of workers and peasants in China in order to boost export revenues that line the pockets of rising propertied layers and the privileged state and party bureaucracy in the new capitalist mandarinate. They've done so at the same time they are intensifying exploitation of toilers across Africa, Asia, and other parts of the world to accumulate capital in China.

By the end of 2008 US imperialism will have spent some

$900 billion on its wars in Afghanistan and Iraq, and the figures will head well into the trillions as the bloodletting continues. On top of that, the US rulers have waved the bloody shirt of 9/11 again and again in order to nearly double their overall war spending (they call it a "defense" budget)—from $308 billion in 2001 to nearly $600 billion in 2008. How are these wars being paid for? They're financed by debt.

In fact, for the first time in American history, the US ruling class is waging a major multifront, multiyear war without patriotic appeals for "sacrifice"—without drastically cutting back government domestic spending, imposing steep new taxes, or pressing "victory" bonds on working people and the middle classes. This time, at least for a while, the "victory" bonds are being bought by capitalists and other wealthy individuals and institutions in the United States, Japan, China, and many other places.

Part III
How the Clintons
Cooked the Books
(May 2008)

PART III

How the Clintons Cooked the Books

(MAY 2008)

PRIOR TO BILL CLINTON'S inauguration in January 1993, capitalism had been hit by two deep recessions: in 1974–75 (the first synchronized slump in the imperialist countries since the Great Depression of the 1930s), and again in 1981–82, with a couple of explosive bursts of inflation during those years. Working people faced not only steeply rising prices and meat and gasoline "shortages," but also mounting joblessness at the same time.

Even using Washington's own deceptive statistics, the official unemployment rate shot above 10 percent in 1982–83. Inflation hit close to 15 percent in 1980. The interest rate on the thirty-year Treasury (the "long bond") reached nearly 15 percent in 1981, and the so-called "prime" rate used as a peg for home equity, auto, and other "consumer" loans peaked at 21 percent.

During the Clinton years, the employing class in the United States moved aggressively to counteract downward pressure on its profit margins. The bosses held down wage increases, counting on inflation to sharply cut real wages and benefit payments. They sped up production, lengthened the workweek, and increased part-time and temporary labor.

At the service of US finance capital and its bondholders, Clinton doggedly pursued a federal "budget surplus" too. A tax windfall from the late 1990s "tech stock" mania was a substantial contributing factor. And temporary reductions in military spending made possible by the disintegration of the Soviet Union (and reemergence of Russia) along with the collapse of the Warsaw Pact resulted in what the US rulers trumpeted as a "peace dividend." Clinton cut the number of US active duty troops by almost 25 percent over his eight years in office, as Washington began a transformation of its global military "footprint" in preparation for wars to come. The US government's war budget as a proportion of GDP was trimmed by 37 percent.[*]

But the Clintons' White House didn't use the savings for "the people," as it claimed it would. In fact, the "peace dividend" ended up more accurately as a domestic "class-war dividend." The Clintons' White House and Congress reduced federal expenditures on Social Security and related payments, education, veterans benefits, public transportation, scientific research. In fact, every major category of government spending was cut except health and Medicare (organized as a boon to insurance companies, HMOs, and other medical businesses), agriculture (more fat subsidies for capitalist farmers and agribusiness), and "justice" (billions for additional and more heavily armed cops, and for courts, prisons, surveillance modernization,

---

[*] After the September 11, 2001, attacks, US military spending—in real terms, adjusted for inflation—roughly doubled over the next decade and a half under the George W. Bush and Barack Obama administrations.

and death chambers).

The upswing in the business cycle over that period was lengthy by past standards, lasting ten years until the opening of the 2001 recession. But it wasn't based on an increase of capacity-expanding capital investment, drawing more and more workers into new or refurbished plants, mines, and mills and greatly increasing the production of salable goods. Instead, that upturn was the product of piling up an enormous mountain of debt and a giant increase in speculative derivative "debt instruments"—a toxic mix that exploded in the new millennium with the financial crisis and economic contraction that are just beginning.

Lending a hand to big banks

Long before that collapse of US capitalism's financial house of cards, the Clinton administration had lent a helping hand to big banks by eliminating regulations they and other moneyed interests deemed "inconvenient."

In 1999 Treasury Secretary Robert Rubin, formerly cochairman of Goldman Sachs, and his deputy, Lawrence Summers, presided over the repeal of the Glass-Steagall Act, which US rulers had imposed in 1933 in response to the wave of bank failures early in the Great Depression. The ruling class had used Glass-Steagall, among other measures, in order to stabilize the capitalist system by requiring a complete separation between, on the one hand, commercial banks and, on the other hand, insurance companies, stock brokerages, and investment banks. (Commercial banks are supposed to make profits by taking in checking and savings deposits from individuals and businesses and lending those funds to businesses, home buyers, and others at higher interest rates. On the other hand, the revenues of so-called investment banks come from raking in fees for "services" to companies and governments in raising capital by issuing bonds, stocks, and other highly risky "financial products"—increasingly including mergers and acquisitions, in hopes of stemming sagging profit rates, as well as "in-house" leveraged speculation using their own funds.)

The wonderfully named Financial Services Modernization Act, which Clinton signed into law in November 1999, facilitated breaching that wall, accelerating and magnifying the results of the operations of finance and money capital. Mergers of deposit banks, investment banks, brokerages, and insurance companies proliferated. Above all, the floodgates were opened to a massive expansion of so-called derivatives, "securitized" debts, "off-balance-sheet" and "shadow" banking operations—in short, complex bets that the capitalist financial boom and mammoth acquisition of US Treasury debt by China, Japan, and other countries would keep going onward and upward. Smaller and smaller amounts of collateral—sometimes little or none—stood behind ever more leveraged loans, with fewer and fewer provisions of any kind to cover the skyrocketing risk.

A case in point is Citigroup, one of the largest US banks. The Clinton administration's Financial Services Modernization Act became law shortly after Citigroup had been formed in 1998 through the merger of Citicorp (then the largest US commercial bank), the giant Travelers insurance company, and the Salomon Smith Barney investment house. It was a blissful marriage, but without repeal of Glass-Steagall, an annulment would have been legally required within two years.

In July 1999 Rubin turned the reins of Clinton's Treasury over to Summers, who then, in return, shepherded the bill through Congress and hailed it as "the foundation for a 21st-century financial system." Barely four months later, in October 1999, Rubin shamelessly took an initially $40-million-per-year job as chairman of Citigroup's executive committee! Not for nothing did many tag the Clintons' new law the "Citigroup Authorization Act."

Rubin continued to occupy that position until 2009, as Citigroup took write-offs and losses of more than $40 billion—yes, billion—from derivatives and other "debt instruments" gone sour. So much for the "magic" of a former Goldman Sachs bond trader in face of the law of labor value!

Manipulating gold prices

The Clinton administration actively worked to keep world gold prices low, thus helping to maintain a "strong dollar" and to keep interest rates relatively low. Among other means, the White House encouraged the International Monetary Fund and Washington's rival imperialist governments (not itself, of course) to publicly sell off their bullion reserves.

The proceeds from such gold sales, Washington cynically sermonized, could then be used for "debt forgiveness" to "help Third World countries" burdened by onerous interest payments on foreign loans. Testifying before Congress in April 1999, then Deputy Treasury Secretary Summers said this income could be used to support "the world's poorest countries, especially those burdened by unsustainable debt." He pledged that such gold sales could "be conducted in a manner that limits any adverse impact on gold holders, producers, and the gold market."

The upshot of this Clinton administration scam was not long in coming. In May 1999, at what were already the lowest world gold prices since the mid-1970s, Gordon Brown, the United Kingdom's treasury minister, and currently its prime minister, announced that London would soon begin selling fully half its gold reserves. Contrary to Summers's assurance that such sales could be "conducted in a manner that limits any adverse impact," Brown's announcement set off such panic on world markets that gold prices dropped by another 10 percent over the next few weeks to a twenty-year low of $253 per ounce, at which price Brown promptly sold more!

As for helping "the world's poorest countries," it's enough to recall that among the top global gold exporters are semicolonial countries such as Peru, Indonesia, Uzbekistan, Papua New Guinea, Chile, Ghana, Mali, and Tanzania, as well as South Africa—whose revenues from mining and exporting gold and other precious metals were devastated!

Over the next few years, the central banks of the United Kingdom, Switzerland, and Canada sold more than half their gold reserves—at historically low prices—and substantial reserves were sold by other central banks too. *The US Treasury, meanwhile, sold virtually none of its own gold reserves*—which, at nearly 9,000 tons, are by far the world's largest hoard (a quarter of official world gold reserves). Beginning in 2002 gold prices began a slow, and in a few years accelerating, climb. By May 2008 the market value of Washington's reserves had more than tripled from $67 billion to nearly $225 billion.

Now that was a plan to help "the world's poorest countries"! And get the best of your imperialist "friends," to boot!

Are prices rising too slowly?

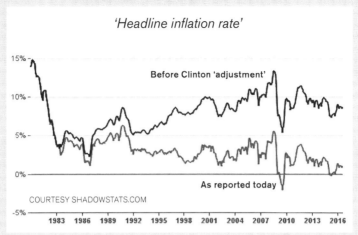

'Headline inflation rate'

Before Clinton 'adjustment'

As reported today

COURTESY SHADOWSTATS.COM

The employers and their government try to convince us that in 2016, cost-of-living adjustments in wages, pensions, and other payments relied on by working people aren't a big deal any more. After all, they say, increases in so-called "headline inflation" are running at "only" 1 percent.

The Federal Reserve board goes so far as to tell us that "inflation" today is "too low." Their "target" is a 2 percent annual increase, almost double today's rate!

Working people, however, know from cash registers and bill payments what's shown by the illustration above. Before Clinton's "revision" (see next page), even the official increase for the prices of things we buy has actually risen much more rapidly than 1 percent. To cite just a few examples from 2015, transit fares increased by more than 5 percent; the price of school lunches 5.5 percent; and health insurance more than 7 percent (with a lot more than that to come!).

Going back to the year 2000, while the government's "headline inflation" has risen 42 percent over that decade and a half, tuition, school fees, and childcare have jumped 124 percent; housing rent 63 percent; health expenses 81 percent; and food and beverages 48 percent.

Faking the cost of living . . .

The Clinton administration also granted a profit bonanza to the employing class by rejiggering the basis on which annual cost-of-living adjustments are calculated in wage payments and Social Security and other benefits to tens of millions of workers and working-class families in the United States. This is a decisive question for working people, as shown by the fact that real wages in this country in 2008—even by government statistics—are some 10 percent lower than they were thirty-five years ago in 1973.

In 1997 the Clinton administration, acting on proposals by a Senate-appointed bipartisan commission, ordered that the government's main yardstick of inflation—the Consumer Price Index (CPI)—henceforth be figured in a way that substantially reduced official price figures. This magic was produced by two tricks in particular.

First, the commission claimed to have unearthed an astounding oversight in the way inflation figures had been figured ever since such statistics had begun being kept decades earlier. In the past, if the price of steak went up, for example, that increase had been reflected in CPI figures. But it suddenly dawned on the commissioners that when steak gets too pricey, "people" simply start buying hamburger instead. So the cost of hamburger should replace the price of steak in the CPI. Shazam! No inflation in meat costs!

In reporting changes in the cost of living, the White House also introduced what it called "hedonics" (a word from the same root as "hedonism"). Lo these many decades, Clinton's commissioners discovered, statisticians had been overlooking the fact that the "pleasure" working people and others derive from the goods we buy increases as new

The US working class is getting smaller

Labor participation rate 2000–2016

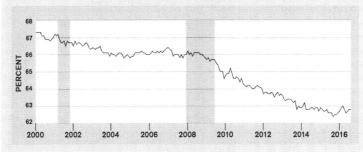

Duration out of a job 2000–2016

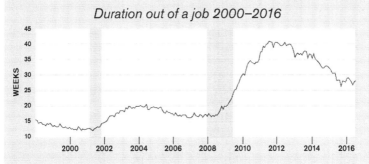

One way the government pretties up its monthly unemployment rate is to keep reducing the percentage of workers (age sixteen and above) it counts as part of the labor force. Since the sharpening of the capitalist crisis in recent years, that share has fallen from more than 66 percent in 2008 to 62.8 percent in August 2016.

That's the lowest since 1977, when the overall rate (for both men and women, that is) was lower, since fewer than half of women sixteen and above were then in the workforce. As fights by women and other working people pushed back sex discrimination in employment, the female labor participation rate rose to more than 60 percent by the mid-1990s and remained roughly at that level until the 2008 crisis, falling below 57 percent since 2014.

(SEE NEXT PAGE)

> The decline in the labor participation rate for men has been particularly sharp, falling from 87 percent in 1950, to 73 percent in 2008, to 69 percent in 2016.
> As for the stretches of time workers go with no job of any kind—an experience burned into the memories of working-class families—the duration averaged 13.5 weeks over the entire six decades between 1948 and 2008. Since then, the average has jumped two and a half times, to nearly eight months.

models are introduced. Cars may become more expensive, but now we can lock or unlock them as we walk across the parking lot. And as we're sending off the next payment for that new computer, we should keep in mind that its speed and memory have expanded—so it's actually getting more and more fun, and thus also "costs" less and less!

What's the bottom line? Whereas the US government's official annual inflation figure in late 2007 was deduced to be 3.2 percent, it would have been 7 percent—*more than double*—calculated by the methods used by every administration since the 1930s. And that means hundreds of billions of dollars in extra profits for the employing class—who are now paying much less in cost-of-living adjustments to workers in wage agreements, as well as Social Security, health, workers comp, and other benefits.

What does that mean in the everyday life of the working majority in the United States? In early 2008, less than half a year after the official inflation figure just cited, the US government announced that its so-called Consumer Price Index was now running a bit higher, at a 4 percent annual rate. But a closer look at that very same price data (even using the government's own crooked methods) reveals that the costs of necessities such as groceries, gasoline, and health care had risen by an average of more than 9 percent over a year earlier.

Yet the Social Security administration announced that in 2008 the roughly 50 million people receiving retirement benefits will get a "cost of living" increase of 2.3 percent in their monthly checks—a measly $24 a month for the average recipient. And tens of millions of other working people will be lucky to get an inflation adjustment of any kind in their take-home pay.

. . . and faking jobless figures too

To help mask the rising social toll of the profit system, the Clinton White House simply erased millions of jobless workers from the government's monthly unemployment figures.

The Clintons learned this disappearing act from a previous Democratic Party role model of morality. During John F. Kennedy's first year in office in 1961, he had worried about the political kickback from a sharp rise in joblessness that year. So he appointed a committee to look for a solution—not a solution to put people back to work, but to do better at keeping up appearances. A few years later the federal government slapped a label on workers who had been unable to find jobs for so long that they had stopped looking. Calling them "discouraged workers," it no longer counted them as being unemployed. Voilà! The "unemployment rate" dropped overnight!

Clinton, who also confronted high joblessness at the opening of his first term, took things a step further. Although since the 1960s "discouraged workers" had no longer been counted as unemployed, they were nonetheless

How the unemployed are disappeared

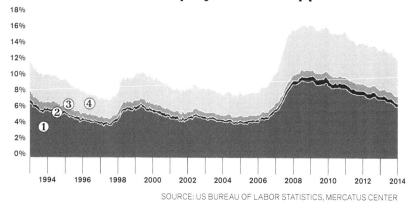

SOURCE: US BUREAU OF LABOR STATISTICS, MERCATUS CENTER

① US government's "official" unemployment rate. This is the percentage of workers counted as part of the civilian labor force who Washington reports are unemployed.

② "Discouraged workers"—Washington's term for unemployed workers who've looked for jobs over the past year but have been unable to find work for so long they haven't bothered to search during the previous month. As a result of a statistical sleight of hand implemented by the Clinton administration, workers who had not looked for work during the past year were simply dropped from what Washington counts as the labor force—thus making roughly half of all "discouraged workers" disappear from government figures.

③ "Marginally attached workers"—Washington's term for unemployed workers who've looked for jobs over the past year but who have not done so during the previous month for any reason. "Discouraged workers" are a relatively small subcategory of "marginally attached workers."

④ Workers working part time who want a full-time job.

included as part of the overall labor force. Evidently that still revealed too much of the actual situation facing working people. So in 1994 the Clinton administration decided that only workers who had been looking for a job within the last year would be counted as part of the workforce. That's how Clinton, with the wave of a statistical wand, disappeared millions more jobless workers!

Despite Washington's deceptive "official" unemployment figures, the labor force participation rate has actually been going down from its post–World War II high point of a little over 67 percent in 2001. That's the best measure available in government records of the percentage of workers *actually holding down a job* or looking for one, and who are thus counted in estimating the "official" unemployment rate. What's more, even among those listed as unemployed in April 2008, almost 20 percent had been jobless for more than six months.

So while government jobless figures are a statistical fiction, the growing millions of workers who've been "disappeared" from the labor force since 2000 are *not*. They are real men and women who've been unable to get a steady job, often for years.

INDEX

Abortion rights, 39–44
  at center of fight against gains
    by women, 39–40
  federal, state, and local
    restrictions on, 41–44
  and Fourteenth Amendment,
    40–41
  Roe v. Wade, 39–41
AFDC (Aid to Families with
  Dependent Children), 29, 35–
  36
Affordable Care Act ("Obamacare,"
  2010), 19
Afghanistan
  US war in (since 2001), 13–14,
    20, 74–76, 81–82
Africa, 14
Age of Turbulence, The (Alan
  Greenspan), 78–80
Agribusiness, subsidies to, 63, 86
Albania, 58
Albright, Madeleine, 20
Amendments to US Constitution
  Fourth Amendment (1791), 66,
    67
  Fourteenth Amendment (1868),
    40, 41, 45, 46
  Fifteenth Amendment (1870),
    45, 46
Anti–Ballistic Missile Treaty
  (1972), 60, 61
Anti-Terrorism and Effective
  Death Penalty Act (1996), 11,
  19, 55, 77

*Are They Rich Because They're
  Smart? Class, Privilege, and
  Learning Under Capitalism*
  (Jack Barnes), 24
Atlantic (magazine), 34

Bangladesh, 14
Bank of America, 79
Barnes, Jack, 9–10, 12, 23–24
Bay of Pigs, US-backed invasion
  (1961), 56–57
Bear Stearns, collapse of, 77–78
Between the World and Me (Ta-
  Nehisi Coates), 34
Black rights, fight for, 12, 29–39,
  41, 45
  See also Amendments to
    US Constitution; Radical
    Reconstruction; Voting rights
Blacks, national oppression of in
  US, 33, 37
  gap in living standards, 32–33
Border police, 54, 65–66
Bosnia, 58, 62
Brown, Gordon, 90
Buchanan, Patrick, 38
Bulgaria, 59
Burger, Warren, 41
Bush, George H.W., 63
Bush, George W., 18, 29, 40, 54,
  56, 58, 66, 72, 78
  and Anti–Ballistic Missile
    Treaty, 60–61
  and death penalty, 48

Also by Jack Barnes

Malcolm X, Black Liberation, and the Road to Workers Power

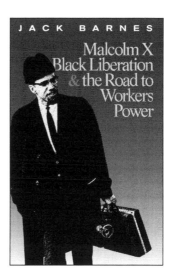

The growing recognition of Malcolm X as a revolutionary leader of working people of all colors, in the US and around the world. And how the revolutionary conquest of state power by a class-conscious vanguard of all origins, millions strong, provides the mightiest weapon to wage the ongoing battle to end Black oppression and every form of exploitation and human degradation.

$20. Also in Spanish, French, Farsi, Arabic, and Greek.

COMPANION VOLUME
The Changing Face of US Politics
Working-Class Politics and the Trade Unions

$24. Also in Spanish, French, Farsi, and Greek.

Cuba and the Coming American Revolution

A book about the struggles of working people in the imperialist heartland, the youth attracted to them, and the example set by the Cuban people that revolution is not only necessary—it can be made. It is about the class struggle in the US, where the revolutionary capacities of workers and farmers are as utterly discounted by the ruling powers as were those of the Cuban toilers. And just as wrongly.

$10. Also in Spanish, French, and Farsi.

The US rulers have begun

Three books for today's spreading and deepening debate among working people looking for a way forward in face of capitalism's global economic and social calamity and wars.

Are They Rich Because They're Smart?

Class, Privilege, and Learning under Capitalism

Jack Barnes

Barnes explains the sharpening class inequalities in the US and takes apart self-serving rationalizations by layers of well-paid professionals that their "intelligence" and schooling equip them to "regulate" the lives of working people who can't be trusted to know our own best interests. In class battles that will be forced on us by the rulers we will transform our attitudes toward life, work, and each other.

$10. Also in Spanish, French, and Farsi.

to fear the working class

Is Socialist Revolution in the US Possible?

A Necessary Debate Among Working People

Mary-Alice Waters

An unhesitating "Yes"—that's the answer by Waters. Possible—but not inevitable. That depends on us. Fighting for a society only working people can create, it's our own capacities we will discover as we cast off the false image of ourselves promoted by those who profit from the exploitation of our labor.

$10. Also in Spanish, French, and Farsi.

Is socialist revolution in the US possible?

A NECESSARY DEBATE AMONG WORKING PEOPLE

MARY-ALICE WATERS

The Clintons' Anti-Working-Class Record

Why Washington Fears Working People

Jack Barnes

Hillary Clinton calls millions of workers "deplorable," "irredeemable." Donald Trump tries to turn us against each other, targeting Mexicans, Muslims, women, whomever. But as Barnes explains, it's their *system* that's deplorable, not *us*! As workers increasingly come to recognize that *capitalism* is the source of the crisis whose burdens we have been made to carry, we'll be able to chart an effective course to resist the rulers' attacks—*and win*.

$10. Also in Spanish, French, and Farsi.

The Clintons' anti-working-class record

WHY WASHINGTON FEARS WORKING PEOPLE

JACK BARNES

The class struggle

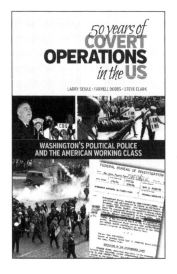

50 Years of Covert Operations in the US
Washington's political police and the American working class
Larry Seigle, Farrell Dobbs, Steve Clark
Traces the decades-long fight by class-conscious workers against efforts to expand presidential powers and build the "national security" state essential to maintaining capitalist rule.
$12. Also in Spanish and Farsi.

"It's the Poor Who Face the Savagery of the US 'Justice' System"
The Cuban Five talk about their lives within the US working class
In a 2015 interview, five Cuban revolutionaries framed up by the US government and imprisoned for 16 years talk about their lives as part of the US working class. And prospects for Cuba's socialist revolution today. Includes 24 pages of photos.
$15. Also in Spanish and Farsi.

Malcolm X Talks to Young People
"The young generation of whites, Blacks, browns, whatever else there is—you're living at a time of revolution," Malcolm said in December 1964. "And I for one will join in with anyone, I don't care what color you are, as long as you want to change this miserable condition that exists on this earth." Four talks and an interview given to young people in the last months of Malcolm's life.
$15. Also in Spanish, French, Farsi, and Greek.

in the United States

Teamster Politics
Farrell Dobbs

A central leader of the battles records how Minneapolis Teamster Local 544 combatted FBI and other government frame-ups in the 1930s; organized the unemployed; mobilized labor opposition to US imperialism's entry into World War II; and fought to lead labor and its allies on an independent working-class political course.
$19. Also in Spanish.

Capitalism's Long Hot Winter Has Begun
Jack Barnes

Published as the storm clouds of the 2008 financial crisis were forming, Barnes explains that today's global capitalist crisis is but the opening stage of decades of economic, financial, and social convulsions and class battles. Class-conscious workers, he writes, confront this historic turning point for imperialism with confidence, drawing satisfaction from being "in their face" as we chart a revolutionary course to take power. In *New International* no. 12.
$16. Also in Spanish, French, Farsi, Arabic, and Greek.

Puerto Rico: Independence Is a Necessity
Rafael Cancel Miranda

One of five Puerto Rican Nationalists imprisoned by Washington in 1954 for more than 25 years speaks out on the brutal reality of US colonial domination, the campaign to free Puerto Rican political prisoners, the example of Cuba's socialist revolution, and the ongoing struggle for independence.
$6. Also in Spanish and Farsi.

Also from Pathfinder

The Communist Manifesto
Karl Marx, Frederick Engels
Founding document of the modern
revolutionary workers movement,
published in 1848. Why communism
is not a set of preconceived principles
but the line of march of the working
class toward power—a line of march
"springing from an existing class struggle,
a historical movement going on under
our very eyes."
$5. Also in Spanish, French, Farsi, and
Arabic.

The Truth About Yugoslavia
Why Working People Should Oppose Intervention
George Fyson, Argiris Malapanis,
Jonathan Silberman
How the US rulers, in collaboration with their
NATO allies and rivals, used deadly bombs and
cruise missiles to finish off the Yugoslav Revolution's
conquest of national unification. In the process,
Washington reinforced its place as the dominant
"European" military power.
$10. Also in Greek.

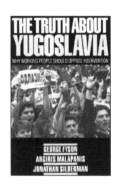

Lenin's Final Fight
Speeches and Writings, 1922–23
V.I. Lenin
In 1922 and 1923, V.I. Lenin, central leader of the
world's first socialist revolution, waged what was to
be his last political battle. At stake was whether that
revolution, and the international movement it led,
would remain on the proletarian course that had
brought workers and peasants to power in October
1917.
$20. Also in Spanish and Greek.

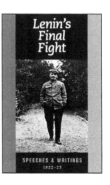

Cuba and Angola
Fighting for Africa's
Freedom and Our Own
Fidel Castro, Raúl Castro,
Nelson Mandela, and others

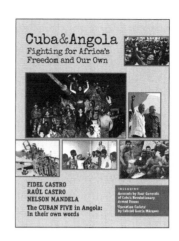

In March 1988, the army of South
Africa's apartheid regime was dealt a
crushing defeat by Cuban, Angolan, and
Namibian combatants in Angola. Here
leaders and participants tell the story of
the 16-year-long internationalist mission
that strengthened the Cuban Revolution
as well.
$12. Also in Spanish.

Revolutionary Continuity
Marxist Leadership in the United States
The Early Years, 1848–1917
Farrell Dobbs

"Successive generations of proletarian revolutionists
have participated in the movements of the working
class and its allies and sought to steer them along the
correct path.... Marxists today owe them not only
homage for their deeds. We also have a duty to learn
where they went wrong as well as what they did right
so their errors are not repeated."—*Farrell Dobbs*
$20

The Revolution Betrayed
What Is the Soviet Union and Where Is It Going?
Leon Trotsky

In 1917 workers and peasants of Russia were the
motor force for one of the deepest revolutions
in history. Yet within ten years a political
counterrevolution by a privileged social layer whose
chief spokesperson was Joseph Stalin was being
consolidated. The classic study of the Soviet workers
state and its degeneration.
$20. Also in Spanish, Farsi, and Greek.

Opening Guns of World War III: Washington's Assault on Iraq
Jack Barnes

Washington's murderous 1991 war on Iraq heralded conflicts among imperialist powers, growing capitalist crisis, and spreading wars. Working people in the region—from the Kurds, to Palestine and Israel, to Iran, Iraq, and Syria—are fighting for space to defend national rights and class interests. In *New International* no. 7.
$14. Also in Spanish, French, and Farsi.

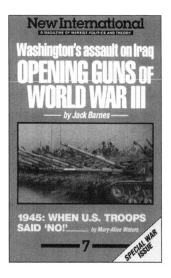

Maurice Bishop Speaks
The Grenada Revolution and Its Overthrow, 1979–83

The triumph of the 1979 revolution in the Caribbean island of Grenada under the leadership of Maurice Bishop gave hope to millions throughout the Americas. Invaluable lessons from the workers and farmers government defeated by a Stalinist-led coup in 1983.
$25

Women's Liberation and the African Freedom Struggle
Thomas Sankara

"There is no true social revolution without the liberation of women," explains the leader of the 1983–87 revolution in the West African country of Burkina Faso.
$8. Also in Spanish, French, and Farsi.

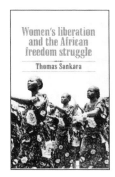

Cuba's Socialist Revolution

Women in Cuba
The Making of a Revolution
Within the Revolution
Vilma Espín, Asela de los Santos, Yolanda Ferrer

The integration of women in the ranks and leadership of the Cuban Revolution was not an aberration. It was inseparably intertwined with the proletarian course of the leadership of the revolution from the start. This is the story of how that revolution transformed the women and men who made it.
$20. Also in Spanish and Greek.

U.S. Imperialism
Has Lost the Cold War
Jack Barnes

Contrary to imperialist expectations with the collapse of regimes claiming to be communist across Eastern Europe and the USSR, the Cuban Revolution did not follow suit. Cuban working people and their leadership have continued to show the world what "socialist revolution" means. In *New International* no. 11.
$16. Also in Spanish, French, Farsi, and Greek.

Playa Girón/Bay of Pigs
Washington's First Military Defeat in the Americas
Fidel Castro, José Ramón Fernández

In fewer than 72 hours of combat in April 1961, Cuba's revolutionary armed forces defeated a US-organized invasion by 1,500 mercenaries. In the process, the Cuban people set an example for workers, farmers, and youth the world over that with political consciousness, class solidarity, courage, and revolutionary leadership, one can stand up to enormous might and seemingly insurmountable odds—*and win*.
$22. Also in Spanish.

PATHFINDER AROUND THE WORLD

Visit our website for a complete list of titles and to place orders

www.pathfinderpress.com

PATHFINDER DISTRIBUTORS

UNITED STATES
(and Caribbean, Latin America, and East Asia)

Pathfinder Books, 306 W. 37th St., 13th Floor
New York, NY 10018

CANADA

Pathfinder Books, 7107 St. Denis, Suite 204
Montreal, QC H2S 2S5

UNITED KINGDOM
(and Europe, Africa, Middle East, and South Asia)

Pathfinder Books, 2nd Floor, 83 Kingsland High Street
Dalston, London, E8 2PB

AUSTRALIA
(and Southeast Asia and the Pacific)

Pathfinder, Level 1, 3/281–287 Beamish St., Campsie, NSW 2194
Postal address: P.O. Box 164, Campsie, NSW 2194

NEW ZEALAND

Pathfinder, 188a Onehunga Mall, Onehunga, Auckland 1061
Postal address: P.O. Box 3025, Auckland 1140

Join the Pathfinder Readers Club
to get 15% discounts on all Pathfinder
titles and bigger discounts
on special offers.
Sign up at www.pathfinderpress.com
or through the distributors above.
$10 a year